Regaining Faith After Boston:

An Insider's Views

by

Sharen Meyers

1726 Evergreen Street
St. Charles, IL 60174

ISBN 1-56794-119-2
Cat. #C-2438

PUBLISHED BY
STAR BIBLE PUBLICATIONS
Fort Worth, Texas 76182

Dedication

This book is dedicated to Tammy, Laura Jane, Lisa, Tara, Ada, and Bev — women whose faith and compassion have inspired me to thirst for a relationship with our Father.

I also wish to thank the following people for their help in making this book possible:

— Dr. Sarah Chambers, Paul Vander Sande, Tammy Henderson, and Kristina Sloniger for their helpful insights, suggestions, and critique of this manuscript.

— Kim Adamson for sharing her photography.

— Jerry Jones for the scope of his ministry and the generosity of his heart.

— Judy Lopez for her constant friendship and "sideline cheering" through the bright as well as the dark periods of my life.

— And especially to my husband, Larry and stepdaughter, Jillian, who have always given me love, support, and confidence in everything I've ever done or dreamed of doing.

About the Author:

Sharen Meyers was converted through a campus ministry while attending Louisiana State University (Baton Rouge) in 1979. The campus ministry began to follow the Boston Movement and she was part of it for eight years. She played an active role for five years and struggled with it for three years until she moved to St. Charles, Illinois in 1986. Both Sharen and her husband, Larry are active in their church. Sharen's future plans include studying for her MSW in the fall of 1997 and to continue writing and speaking at retreats, workshops, etc.

CONTENTS

*Chapter Notes at End of Chapters

Christians *Can* Be Abusive

"What a wonderful God we have—he is the Father of our Lord Jesus Christ, the source of every mercy, and the one who so wonderfully comforts and strengthens us in our hardships and trials. And why does he do this? So that when others are troubled, needing our sympathy and encouragement, we can pass on to them this same help and comfort God has given us."   *2 Cor 1: 3,4   LB*

In the fall of 1979, I joined a church I had always dreamed of attending; within the next few years I would only dream of escaping. I envied those who left before me; I pitied those who joined. But I felt trapped. Trapped within something that was larger than life; something I was afraid to embrace yet terrified to lose.

By the time I left the Boston Movement eight years later, I was battling depression. I was afraid of God. One night I drank 1½ bottles of wine to keep from doing anything worse. I wanted to die but the threat of Hell kept me from suicide. The next morning I knew I had to make a change; I could not go on like this.

I moved to a new city in a different state. I was much happier, but one problem persisted: Boston was still with me. I made the physical break, but I was emotionally tied to the teachings that had been so thoroughly engraved. To resolve the conflict (so I reasoned), I walked away from God, the Bible and above all, the church.

When I began to hear of others leaving the Movement, their stories sounded strangely familiar, such as the following:

- A Christian's (biological) brother is killed in a car accident and his "mentor" tells him his brother is in Hell because he didn't confront him with the Gospel enough.

- A minister tells a bloodied woman her husband wouldn't beat her if she were more submissive.

- A spiritually mature Christian is told he cannot be promoted to the staff position as he was promised because he does not smile enough.

- A teenager is sexually assaulted by a popular youth minister. He is arrested, convicted and jailed. The church blamed the teenager for the loss of the minister.

- A man disagrees with a church teaching and as he begins to explain his reasons, the minister tells him to stop being divisive and rebellious against the Spirit.

- A woman confronts a male member of the church about his inappropriate behavior and is rebuked for trying to "teach a man."

- An overweight woman is told her inability to lose weight is "proof" she had never become a Christian and did not have the Holy Spirit to help her.

- A couple is told they can no longer date since one has leadership potential and the other does not. The one without potential, it is explained, would hinder God's work.

As I heard these stories, I recognized *their* situations as being abusive. Then I realized they were similar to *my own*. My depression began to lift and I felt a sense of relief. Relief because maybe the God I learned to dread was *not* the God of the Bible. Relief because maybe I was *not* a "useless" person. Relief because I was not alone in believing the practices of the Movement were excessive, and yes, abusive.

You might be reading this because you were involved with the discipling ministries of the Boston Movement and you're not sure you can trust God or Christians anymore. You studied the Bible, played an active role in the church, opened your life to others and now feel burned. Betrayed. Confused. The church was not what it had appeared to be. You feel like the rug was pulled out from under you. Maybe you still feel the sting of raw emotions and unanswered questions. And you hurt.

Or maybe you know someone from the Boston Movement you'd like to help but you're not familiar with it. You're not sure what to say, how much to say, or if you should even try. Their reactions to religious topics might be contradictory; one day explosive, another day grateful. They may bounce between confiding in you and keeping you an arm's length away. You're not sure if you should put the brakes on or keep going.

Fortunately for us, the Bible records what Jesus had to say to and about the abusive religious leadership in His day. Over two thousand years later, the same words can aptly describe the Boston Movement. In Matthew 23 He told the crowds, "It may be all right to do what they say, but above anything else, don't follow their example. For they don't do what they tell you to do. They load you with impossible demands that they themselves don't even try to keep." (Matt 23:3,4 LB). And in Mark, Jesus said, "These people speak very prettily about the Lord but they have no love for him at all. Their worship is a farce, for they claim that God commands the people to obey their petty rules." (Mark 7:6,7 LB)

Jesus did more than identify and warn abusive leaders and their followers; He gave them the solution to such heavy-handed religion. "Come to me and I will give you rest—all of you who work so hard beneath a heavy yoke. Wear my yoke—for it fits perfectly—and let me teach you; for I am gentle and humble, and you shall find rest for your souls; for I give you only light burdens." (Matt 11:28-30 LB) These passages will be explored in more detail in the following chapters.

This booklet will not answer every question you may have, but you will gain some insights to aid you in getting help or being of help. If you would like further study, I have included a list of recommended reading in the back of this booklet. The following chapters include what I have learned through counseling, personal Bible study, reading, and conversations with others of the same experience. I am not an expert, a counselor or a theologian. I am an ex-Boston member. More than that, to paraphrase Luke 15, I am the parable of the lost daughter:

"... She got together all she had, set off for a distant country and there squandered her wealth ... when she came to her senses ... she got up and went to her father. But while she was still a long way off, her father saw her and was filled with compassion for her; he ran to his daughter, threw his arms around her and kissed her ... He said, 'Let's have a feast and celebrate. For this daughter of mine was dead and is alive again; she was lost and is found.' So they began to celebrate ..." (Lk 15:11-24 NIV)

When I became a Christian, I was given considerable wealth in knowing my Father and my God. I lost all He gave me as I tried to uphold a religion. When I saw how far away I was from Him, I was afraid to go back. I wasn't sure He would even want me back. With great apprehension I began the walk home. True to (His) form, He spotted me before I saw Him and ran to be the first to welcome me home.

In His loving embrace, I discovered what I had forgotten about my Father: His strong arms are gentle enough to hold me. My Father's arms belong to me because I'm His daughter. And I belong in His arms.

If you are a wandering son or daughter of God, I want to say this to you: you can come home again. It doesn't matter what you've heard, what you've done or where you've gone; the Father is searching the road for your return. He'll unload the baggage, clean the sores, and heal the wounds. He'll clothe you, feed you, and celebrate your return.

No matter how far away you may be, it begins with your first step on the road home. I know what our Father will do; as soon as He spots you hobbling down that path, His heart will nearly burst with compassion and excitement and He will run to welcome you.

You may find it hard to believe that such a reception or such a Father exists, but it does and He does. He celebrated my return and He will yours too. So will I.

C'mon, let's go home; our Father is waiting.

What is the Boston Movement?

If you have never heard of the Boston Movement, you may be surprised at the extent of their ministry. To my knowledge, they have planted or "reconstructed" churches in nearly every major American city, including New York, Chicago, Dallas, Los Angeles, Atlanta, Providence, Phoenix, Washington D.C., San Francisco, San Diego, Orlando, Miami, Columbia, and Denver. Outside the U.S. they have developed churches in Mexico City, Toronto, Tokyo, Sydney, Paris, London, Brussels, Moscow, Buenos Aires, Fiji, Manila, Hong Kong, Munich, Cairo, Seoul, Helsinki, Bombay, and Johannesburg to name a few. Sunday morning attendance has ranged from 400-6000 in these churches. (Whether or not they still do, I'm not sure.)

Boston's goal is to reach the world in one generation; meaning, *this* generation. They might actually do it.

A Short History of the Boston Movement

The roots of the Boston Movement begin in the 1970's with the Crossroads Church of Christ led by Chuck Lucas in Gainesville, Florida. (Boston's leaders tend to "overlook" or deny this since both the Crossroads church and Chuck Lucas oppose what Boston is doing.) Among the Churches of Christ, it was referred to as the "Crossroads Movement." Focused on college campuses as a way to reach the world, they developed an evangelistic outreach program through "Soul Talks." These "Talks" were hour long Bible studies designed to help people understand how the Bible relates to today.

Influenced by the "discipleship" or "shepherding" movement, (started in the early 70's by leaders in the charismatic movement), Crossroads popularized the concept of the "prayer partner" relationship as the way to help Christians mature and grow in their faith, referred to as "discipling." After someone became a Christian, he/she met weekly with an older Christian to be "trained in the faith." During the meeting time, the older Christian would ask about the other's life, answer any questions, issue challenges for growth, and pray with the younger Christian. In time, the younger disciple would then be ready to disciple others, who would disciple others to disciple others and so on.

Through the Crossroads ministry, many people were converted, trained and sent throughout the U.S. as ministers, campus ministers and women's counselors. One of these converts was Kip McKean, who later became the leader of the Boston Movement. McKean was converted through the campus "Soul Talks" and was trained by Chuck Lucas for the ministry. From 1975 to 1979, he was a campus minister, first at Northeastern Christian College near Philadelphia, then at Eastern Illinois University in Charleston, Illinois. In 1979 a small church in Lexington, Massachusetts asked him to become their campus minister and pulpit minister. He accepted.

In his first year, that small church of 30 believers baptized over 100 people. Growth snowballed each year. The following year was over 200, then over 400, over 600, over 900, over 1000 and then over 1600 baptisms in one year! Expanding upon some of the Crossroads' techniques, the nearly extinct Lexington Church of Christ blossomed into the Boston Church of Christ with Sunday attendance nearing the 5000 mark. Worship services are still held at the Boston Garden, home of the Celtics basketball team.

Such incredible success captured the notice of everyone in the ministry; no one had done so much in such a small amount of time before. Kip was often invited to speak at seminars and conferences to answer the question: "How did you do that?" Boston was willing to teach anyone who was interested, and thus, the "Boston Movement" was born. As a "multiplying" or "discipleship ministry," Boston converts, trains (disciples), and sends out others to do the same in her effort to reach the world. People from all over the States moved there, including other successful ministers, to be retrained. Those who didn't move followed Boston's example by implementing her methods.

Prayer partners evolved into discipleship partners with everyone assigned to be under one person and over another(s). The discipler was considered one's "covering" in the Lord to help keep him out of sin. Partners were expected to meet weekly, but have daily contact. Soul Talks were renamed Bible Talks. (Boston had over 300 ongoing weekly Talks.) Door knocking gave way to shopping malls, sporting and community event "blitzes." (This involved going to where the crowds were and inviting every person we could stop to Bible Talks and/or church.) Boston's "14-Day" study was used with non-Christians instead of the book of Romans. (This was an organized plan of studies and social "outings" designed to bring someone to a decision about Christ within two weeks.)

In her efforts to restore New Testament Christianity, Boston developed "house churches." During the week, services were held at a leader's house and members met in their assigned "zones." On Sundays all the believers came back together as a whole Body at the Celtic's arena. This inducted a new ladder of leadership, reflecting the advice Jethro gave Moses (Exodus 18) to select a group of men to help oversee the Israelites.

Leadership began with the assistant Bible Talk leader, then Bible talk leader (over 10's), the house leader (over 50's) who was over several Bible Talks, and then the zone leader (over 100's) who was over several house churches. Leading a zone was usually a paid, full-time staff position and the stepping stone to becoming an evangelist or women's counselor. (Zone leaders who were not yet evangelists or counselors were called "interns.") The same pattern was established in the churches in Chicago, San Francisco, New York and other large cities.

Boston started to develop and send their own "Mission Teams" to other states and countries to plant churches. Only those trained by Boston were allowed to go or hold a position of leadership. The plan was to place a group of disciples in each key metropolitan area of the world who would develop a church, called "pillar churches," which would in turn send out more disciples for church plantings until the entire nation was evangelized. The key churches were called "pillar churches" because the rest of the Movement would be directed through them and be built into a "world brotherhood."

Boston encouraged their people to sell homes, take out loans, or to do "whatever it would take" to tithe more sacrificially so "the work of winning the world in this generation could be realized." The congregations took the goal seriously and churches were planted across the States as planned. All affiliated churches came under the direct control of the "mother" church, Boston. This is why the term "Boston Movement" refers to more than just the Boston Church of Christ; it refers to all the churches planted or reconstructed by her. In fact, in a speech to the Boston Church of Christ on May 6, 1990, Kip McKean said: "The Boston Church is not just any church. It is the Jerusalem of God's modern day movement." [1]

McKean is the undisputed leader of the Boston Movement. Al Baird, an elder and evangelist for Boston wrote in the January 7, 1990 issue of the *Boston Bulletin*: "God has certainly raised up the McKeans to build the Boston Church and the Movement... We praise God that he has raised up Kip to lead the Movement in our generation." McKean and those who follow him believe God has placed him in the role of the Apostle Paul to "make disciples of all nations."

For the Boston churches, to be saved means you had to be a disciple of Jesus *before* baptism or you are still lost. (Qualifications of a "disciple" will be explained in the next chapter.) If this was not your belief and commitment at your baptism, then you only got wet. You are still separated from God. As a result, hundreds of people submitted to being rebaptized by the Boston church, including elders, ministers, counselors, and other leaders who were converted through Crossroads and Boston.

Calling Out the Remnant

In the 1980's, Boston began to call herself the "Remnant;" that is, the only ones faithful to God, based on Isaiah 10:21-22: "Only a remnant will return." The belief is that "God takes the few faithful ones and separates them from the unfaithful to have a purified people devoted to him."[2] This resulted in more people moving to join the ranks of the "faithful." In 1986, Boston called all Churches of Christ to congregational repentance. She invited them to join her in restoring the New Testament church and to learn how to multiply disciples. Any church willing to be under her leadership in a "reconstruction" could unite with them. The migration to Boston churches continued to grow while she tried to "glean all the remaining faithful" into her fold. The cities refusing Boston's invitation were targeted for future church plantings.

During the reconstruction process (based on the reconstruction of Jerusalem detailed in the Old Testament book of Nehemiah), the church was renamed according to the city it was located in and the leaders replaced by Boston trained evangelists. The displaced leaders were then sent to other Boston ministries for at least a year of training and discipleship. Once there, the training leaders had to review the commitment they made at baptism with the strong possibility of being rebaptized. In addition, they were expected to "submit fully" to their assigned discipleship partner, or get out. They were not ready to be sent out again until the Boston leaders felt their retraining was complete. Usually it was not back to their original church.

Many churches, including Crossroads, have taken a strong stand against the practices and teachings of the Boston Movement. These churches, as well as former members within the Movement, have asked her leaders to meet with them to discuss the issues that separate them. Boston has declined these invitations. She considers her critics as "fallen," "uncommitted," and "divisive." Boston churches point to their numbers (at one time, the Boston Sunday attendance was nearly 7,000) as proof they are right and the lack of growth in the mainline churches as proof they are wrong. Membership in a church not agreeing with her teachings, she warns, "can lead you to Hell."

The World Plan

Late in 1988, Kip McKean resigned as the Boston Church of Christ evangelist to become the "World Missions Evangelist." His plan was to follow Paul's example and focus on discipling the lead couples (of the Movement) and the pillar churches they serve.[3] McKean divided the world into "sectors" and hand-picked the men he wanted over those areas. They were Douglas Arthur (British Commonwealth and Scandinavia), Steve Johnson (Eastern U.S., Caribbean, and Africa), Randy McKean (New England and Europe), Phil Lamb (Central and South America), Frank Kim (Far East), Scott Green (China), Marty Fuqua (Midwest-Western U.S., Canada and Russia; Tom Brown was the original leader over this area but left the ministry due to "personal spiritual problems"), Al Baird (Middle East), and Bob Gempel (Finances).

These "world sector leaders" are responsible for the evangelization of their geographical areas, or "sectors." Each sector has a "pillar church" and this church (more specifically, the world sector leader) has authority over all the churches in her region. Collectively, they make the decisions in setting the direction for the churches. All of these men answer to and are discipled by Kip McKean. In McKean's words: "... since leadership in God's movement is by relationship, I felt one of the primary requirements for the "focused few" would be that *I had personally trained and discipled them.*"(italics mine, SM).[4] In turn, the sector leaders disciple the leaders in their areas and direct the ongoings of the churches. That is, as Kip directs them. Boston has lots of long-distance discipling.

The Boston Movement in the 90's

In 1990, the McKeans moved to Los Angeles to develop a "super church" as a model for the rest of the churches to follow. (L.A. is one of the U.S. pillar churches). They were also discipling the Fuquas as world sector leaders to replace the Browns. But regardless of where he lives, Kip McKean remains as the "world evangelist" and director of the entire Boston Movement.

In the early 90's, some of Boston's leaders, (Kip McKean, Randy McKean, Al Baird), admitted that there "had been some wrong teaching," in the Movement, particularly in the area of authority. However, they did not say what that wrong teaching was, how they realized it was wrong, and what the correct teaching would now be. In following their subsequent teachings and practices, their "wrong teachings" and views have not changed. (If you would like further study on this, this is well documented in Jerry Jones, *What Does the Boston Movement Teach?*, Vol. 2 and 3.)

In 1992, the 103 Boston churches broke away from the mainline Church of Christ and is now called the International Church of Christ. Attendance at that time in the Movement churches was over 50,000 and membership nearly 38,000.[5]

Whether she is known as the Boston Movement, Multiplying Ministries, Discipleship Ministries, Restoring Ministries, or the International Church of Christ, the major controversial areas still remain in her teachings on authority, baptism, discipling, the autonomy of churches, and the role of Kip McKean. She continues to refuse to meet with any of her critics for discussion on any of these topics.

One problem Boston can no longer ignore, cover up, or blame on "bad hearts" is the poor retention rate within her churches. They lose nearly as many members as they gain. In March 1990, Al Baird, Boston's lead evangelist at the time (Kip McKean had moved to Los Angeles), admitted in his sermon that although they had baptized over 1500 people in 1989, they had only grown numerically by 300! That means over 1200 people left the Boston Church of Christ in one year! In a two year analysis (1990-91), the Boston church baptized 39,986 people but only grew by 16,350! In those two years she lost 23,636 believers! That leaves a drop out rate of 56%! In one city! [6]

The Boston Movement has many fallen leaders and wounded people who are not sure what to do with the disillusionment, the questions, the scars, and the pain leftover from their time in the ministry. Members leave because of the pressure to produce, the discouragement in not being able to meet the expectations placed on them, the hurts inflicted through the discipling relationships, and the major doctrinal errors as listed earlier. Of those who leave, some join other churches, some start new churches, and some are doubtful if they will ever attend church again. Some, like me, reject their faith.

My story at least has a happy ending; some don't.

[1] Jerry Jones' *What Does The Boston Movement Teach?* WDTBMT Vol. 1, p. 26.

[2] Kip McKean, "Revolution Through Restoration," *Upside Down*, April 1992; entire article reprinted in Jerry Jones' *WDTBMT?* Vol. 3, pp. 103-114

[3] *Boston Bulletin*, June 26, 1988; reprinted in Jerry Jones' *WDTBMT?* Vol. 1, p. 106

[4] Kip McKean, *"Revolution Through Restoration,"* J.J *WDTBMT?* Vol.3, p. 110

[5] Jerry Jones' WDTBMT? Vol. 3, p.111 and Time, "Keepers of the Flock," May 18, 1992

[6] Jerry Jones" WDTBMT? Vol. 3, pp. 32-35

Inside Boston

Although I was a part of the Boston Movement, I did not live in Boston or in any of her affiliated city-churches. However, the campus ministry of the church I attended tried to imitate all that Boston did, including her teachings and her methods. That's why I say I am an ex-Boston member. The more successful Boston became, the more our campus ministry tried to follow. This caused severe divisions within the church. Some wanted to be "just like Boston;" some wanted nothing to do with her, and some of us felt there was a happy — and healthy — medium.

The Story of One Follower

My introduction into the Church of Christ was in 1979, the second week of my freshman year at Louisiana State University, through a "Soul Talk." I liked the style of the discussion and was eager to learn more, so I visited the church. I was amazed. Even though I had attended church and read the Bible since I was 8 years old, I had never heard or seen anything like this before.

The congregation assembled in a semi-circle around the pulpit so that when they sang, they smiled and sang to one another instead of staring at the songbook. Many of them stood arm in arm.

Whenever the minister read from the Bible, I could hear what sounded like hundreds of pages turning to read along with him. Many of those sitting around me were taking notes — in notebooks, not pieces of scratch paper. I was intrigued.

After the services, people greeted each other with hugs and smiles, talked, and shared Scriptures with each other. There was no stampede to get out; they wanted to be together. When I left, my heart was on fire.

Along with church and the "Soul Talks," I studied the Bible with another church member. I found some things lacking in my basic knowledge and was baptized in late September of 1979. I was given a copy of "The First Forty Days," (a Bible study guide given to every new believer, based on Israel's 40 years of wandering in the desert), assigned a prayer partner, and encouraged to share my new faith.

When Jack and Nancy Winters (not their real names) became our new campus minister and women's counselor, I thought Nancy was the most refreshing person I had ever met. She often said "encourage" meant "to put courage into" and she epitomized that definition.

I loved to listen to her talk about God because she had a freshness in her Christianity that was captivating. I was often on the edge of my seat as she taught us about a loving God, developing close friendships, being honest with our struggles, dealing with sin and sharing our faith. When she picked me and two others as her first "disciples," I was thrilled and determined to learn everything I could from her. As a group, we were beginning to blossom under their leadership and would do anything they asked of us. We wanted the same type of Christianity they seemed to have. That first year was challenging, but very fun. We looked forward to more of the same.

But then we started watching Boston. We adopted her teachings and practiced her methods. The atmosphere of the ministry began to change. It was not all at once of course; it was subtle, but constant, until it no longer resembled the group I had joined. The campus ministry became a business, not a family.

I was leading one "Bible Talk" and co-leading another, but felt uncomfortable with three things: in actuality, the discussions were only to meet and convert others, not to grow in the faith, as it was so billed and I felt this was deceitful. Secondly, non-Christians consisted of anyone not baptized in our church, and the unspoken rule for the Christians was mandatory attendance (called "support") at the talks. I believed if people were growing in their faith, evangelism would come naturally, without being forced or demanded, but I didn't say anything because I was "in training."

The Soul Talk leaders and co-leaders were required to attend the Friday afternoon leaders' class followed by the leaders' meeting. At class, we studied Biblical characters like David or Nehemiah, or books like *The Masterplan of Evangelism* or *Multiplying Ministries*. These were our "manuals." We were encouraged to be men and women "after God's own heart" (like David) and to "rebuild the walls" of people's lives (like Nehemiah). Greater emphasis was placed on reaching more people by training (i.e., discipling) others to do the same thing. Each semester we were expected to lead more people to Christ than the one before; when we didn't, we were told we were selfish.

In the leaders meetings, we reported the number of visitors at our dorm discussions and the number of one-on-one studies we were having with them. Individual studies were always set up with anyone who visited the discussions. The one-on-one studies were usually two-on-one because we were expected to bring a younger Christian with us to teach them how to study the Bible with others.

My schedule became way too hectic. Church activities packed my week. On Sundays, we had morning and evening services; sometimes classes between services; and after the night service, we had a leader's meeting for the sisters with Nancy; Mondays were studies with non-Christians and door knocking; Tuesdays were Bible Talk; Wednesday was church; Thursdays were meetings with the sisters at my Bible Talk and more Bible studies; Fridays were leaders meetings and classes, followed by Friday night devotional, which lasted until 11 or 12 o'clock; Saturdays were the only nights we were allowed to date and we had to be in by midnight. I was a full-time student, held two part-time jobs, was Secretary of our campus group, President of my dorm and Bible Talk leader. Being a Bible Talk leader involved not only writing the discussions, but also knowing what was going on with each Christian and non-Christian who attended it. In addition, I was to disciple two other Christians and study with non-Christians.

I asked Nancy to be relieved of my leadership position because I could not keep up with it and was not doing a good job. (Once someone began to lead Bible Talks, it was expected every semester; we were given our assigned dorms without being asked if we could or would continue to lead a Talk.) I showed her my schedule, which she no more than glanced at and put aside. Instead of the hoped-for relief of stepping down, she said I needed to deepen my faith and dependency upon God. If I did not continue (with the Bible Talk), I would be lessening God's work and my growth. She reminded me she had worked while in nursing school and lead a Bible Talk but had accomplished more than what I was doing; obviously, I needed more discipline and dedication instead of quitting when it got a little tough. I agreed to continue and left, knowing I would need a miracle to survive. We never talked about it again.

I went to talk to a brother who was highly respected, fruitful, and a post-graduate student. He admitted he regularly used "No Doz" to keep up with everything. I didn't feel like I had much of a solution.

That semester I was continually ill and had debilitating tension headaches. Light would cause terrible pain and there were times I couldn't lift my head. I missed several classes, my grades suffered, and I had to drop some courses. My allergies worsened and I developed asthma. I couldn't wait for the semester to be over so I could have a break.

Each semester felt more intense than the one before. I felt I was drowning.

At the Friday leaders' meetings, the number of visitors to our Bible Talks were compared to each other, to other campus ministries and of course, to Boston. We always lacked in comparison. Then Jack charged us to "clip the wings" of the other Christians' week-ends by "encouraging" them to stay for the Friday night devotional and return for Sunday night services instead of spending the entire weekend at home visiting family. He said our people needed to be committed and be where they could grow. And that was here at the church, specifically, within the campus ministry.

We were given the "Boston checklist" to help us "watch our lives and doctrine closely." The checklist was an examination for "godliness": Did you have a Quiet Time every day? (one hour was the minimum) Have you prayed? Who did you share your faith with today? Are you confessing sins to your discipler? Have you talked with your discipler and disciplee today? We were supposed to do this weekly, if not daily.

If I thought the Friday meetings were drudgery, the Sunday nights with Nancy were worse. We would review the numbers once again and she would berate us for being weak, mediocre, and lazy. Her theme was since no one rises above the leadership, the low numbers of converts and lack of growth among the sisters had to be a result of our poor relationship with God and lack of gratitude for the cross. We needed to deal with the sin in our lives and stop holding God back. Afterwards I would go to the dorm and beg God to show me what sins I was holding onto and stopping His work. It seemed I could never repent enough.

The best meetings we had were the few Nancy did not attend. When we would leave encouraged and motivated, Nancy would counter back the next week with an "I'll believe it when I see it" attitude and we would be deflated again. "No pain, no gain;" "The road to Hell is paved with good intentions;" "Lead, follow, or get out of the way;" "To whom much is given, much is expected;" and "Work hard, love harder" were mottoes I heard constantly.

Sometimes, before our goal-setting sessions, we would go around the table and have to tell each other what we saw as their top two strengths and weaknesses. I hated those sessions. Legalism and perfectionism were listed as my weaknesses nearly every time.

One Sunday afternoon, I tried to have a "Quiet Time" but couldn't stay awake, so I laid down for a nap. Nancy stopped by my dorm room and woke me up. She started to question me about those I was keeping up with and I couldn't answer all her questions. She reminded me "the time was short and I needed to be working."

At the leaders' meeting that night, she blasted us (me) with the need to die to our selfishness. She said we were so busy having God meet our needs and getting our rest that we were letting the world go to Hell. God wasn't pleased with just one or two studies with non-Christians; we should be taking every opportunity to seek the lost the way Jesus did. He sacrificed sleep, He missed meals, and He stopped grieving over the death of John the Baptist so He could help the crowds. At our rate, when God judged our work, we would make it into Heaven with the smell of smoke on our clothes. She reminded us of Tom Brown's three step plan for success: "work, work, work." There were no easy roads, just easy excuses.

Eventually I would numb out at these meetings. I didn't need Nancy to tell me how my weak character stopped others from seeking or growing in the Lord; I believed it myself. She announced that she would no longer spend her time with those who did not have a "discipler's heart." Such a heart translated into someone who would willingly, joyfully, thoroughly, unquestioningly and successfully follow the lead of the discipler. She was planning to concentrate only on those who wanted to grow, instead of wasting her time with lukewarm believers. She had dropped me long ago, so this was no news to me. (Actually, she never discipled me the way she expected us to disciple others, so I'm not sure "dropped" is the proper term.)

Nancy regularly reminded me of how younger Christians were doing so much better than I was and none of them wanted to be like me. I felt ashamed for not "getting it." I thought something was wrong with me. I told myself that if I would really put an effort into things, God would bless me and help me grow. I just never understood why it had to be so hard.

Until the day they moved to a Boston church, Nancy always told me (that is, if she would even acknowledge me) my problem was my "divided heart." Sometimes she would say, "I was reading this verse and it reminded me of you," and it was typically a Proverb about complacency or double-mindedness. If I defended myself, I would be called prideful, so I just accepted it and tried harder. And I would always fail at whatever I did.

At services, if she wanted to speak to me, she would make me wait until she had talked to everyone else before we sat down to talk. Or rather, her to lecture and me to repent. If someone came over to talk to her while we were talking, she would stop our conversation, talk to them and then get back to me. When I would become angry, she responded with how I had no right to feel anger. She knew ours would be a difficult conversation and there were others she needed to fellowship with as well.

The last college function I attended was a Friday night devotional. The brothers were at a men's retreat, so all the college sisters gathered at the campus student center. Nancy asked us to share what our biggest dreams were. Nearly everyone shared something and I said I wanted to go to Russia to help develop a church. The more people talked about what was on their hearts, the more exciting it became. It was very uplifting. After everyone finished, Nancy said all our dreams had one thing in common: none of them took faith to believe in. Any of us could accomplish those on our own; we needed to dream bigger dreams that really caused us to use our faith. I was stunned. How could she know what did or did not take faith for me to believe in? I became angry as I realized she had planned on saying that no matter what we had shared. I felt she had set us up.

I dropped out of college, became part of the single adult group and a workaholic. Work was the only place I felt a sense of worth. At least they liked and appreciated me. Another sister invited me to share an apartment with her and I accepted. She was dutifully warned about not letting my weak character influence her growth, but fortunately, she did not let those comments influence her. She got to know me and we are still friends today.

Two years later, disillusioned and confused about what to believe or not believe, I moved to a new state and what I hoped would be a new beginning. Six years passed before I felt safe in approaching God; two more until I found a healthy and loving church. It's been a long and often painful journey, but I don't regret it.

Characteristics of the Boston Environment

As I read stories of other, more prominent leaders of the Boston Movement and why they left it, I realized that what I experienced was not my imagination. Nor was it simply a case of immaturity in the leaders of my campus ministry. It was just the way the Boston Movement "worked."

I learned to stop feeling guilty over my "unproductivety" in the Movement. Feeling burdened and longing for freedom was not because I had no love for God; rather, it was a normal reaction in response to a heavy religion. Wanting out of the Movement was not because I was attracted to the world, unspiritual, or tangled in some dark, hidden sin (as I was told it was). Wanting out of it was the way I "should" have felt! It was so liberating to know I was "normal!"

If you have a hard time relating to someone from the Boston Movement, please read the rest of this chapter carefully. Understanding the environment in which they were spiritually raised will help you minister to them more effectively.

This is hardly an exhaustive list of characteristics of the Boston churches, but it does describe some of the more common traits. Here's the short list:

Elitism
Legalism
Burdening
Image conscious
Difficult to leave
Kills the wounded
Stresses submission
Autocratic leadership
Lacks formal training
Stresses "total" commitment
Evangelism is the only "fruit"
Holds onto a false basis of authority

The rest of this chapter will explain more about these "trademarks" of Boston. Although they are not in any particular order and some do overlap, the most far reaching trait is the amount of control they exert over their members.

(Note: Although it is more "politically correct" to use the term "he/she," I find it makes reading more difficult. In view of this, I opted to use "he" in the generic sense. Also, much of the material I am using is from the three volumes written by Jerry Jones, *What Does The Boston Movement Teach?* because his work is taken directly from the tapes, articles and bulletins of the Boston churches. Nearly half of his books are reprints of their written material. Dr. Jones taught at Harding University for over 17 years and also served as chairman of the Department of Philosophy and Religion. He moved in 1983 to be part of the Boston Movement and served as an elder in the Boston Church of Christ. He left the Movement in 1987.)

#1 Autocratic leadership

"... they claim that God commands the people to obey their petty rules ... you ignore God's specific orders and substitute your own traditions. You are simply rejecting God's laws and trampling them under your feet for the sake of your tradition." Mark 7: 7-9 LB

A low level of trust and a high level of control exists over the lives of the members. The leaders develop a totalitarian environment and use fear, intimidation, manipulation, and shame to dominate the followers and keep them on "the straight and narrow path." Members are warned about the dangers of being attached to the world, falling away, and becoming complacent. (Complacency is considered worse than falling away). To avoid these pitfalls, they are taught to attend all services, participate in all programs, seek advice for every matter, and live "open, transparent lives."

"The heart is deceitful above all things and beyond cure. Who can understand it?" (Jeremiah 17: 9) is quoted as the reason for their far reaching authority. The premise is no one can fully know himself without being deceived unless the counsel of others is followed. To keep from being deceived, he must have a life that is open to questioning, correcting and directing by another. No boundaries or private areas are allowed to exist or he could be lead into sin. No decision, on any matter, can be made without the advice of others or he might make the wrong decision. However, seeking advice is more than listening to another's opinion and then making his decision; it means taking that advice — regardless. To ask and not accept the advice — or to not ask at all — means he is rebellious and independent. He will be told he has a "bad heart."

He is told when, if, and where he can move (regardless if he wants to or not), which ministry to go into, which job to accept or reject, who he can marry, when and how many children to have, and how much money he should be contributing to the church. The leaders dictate where, when, how long and who he can spend his time with, from friends, to dates, to marriage partners. (This is called "advice" or "discipling.")

If he spends more than the "approved" amount of time with a friend, that friendship will be systematically broken up, usually by multiple talks and "assignments" to disciple or co-lead (a Bible Talk) with other people. For example, my college roommate and I were told not to room together anymore because it was "selfish." We were assigned different dorms and roommates for "the good of the kingdom."

Dating required approval, under the guise of "guidance," for who we were seeing. We were limited to Saturday night double dates and our fellowship time was monitored to ensure we weren't "focused on ourselves." Any phone conversations, other than asking for a date, was frowned upon and we were expected to report any kissing or lustful thoughts.

Kip McKean's words in June 1988 at Denver's Reconstruction says it all:

"... we got to recognize this, in the church, as in the Old Testament, God's people have always been a kingdom and not a democracy. In a democracy you vote, in the kingdom you obey. You know, if there'd been a democracy at the Red Sea, it'd been a disaster. It is God's wisdom to have a kingdom. Amen? And the man that will lead this work, though not perfect, but he is of God, is Preston. And you need to obey in the Lord. The only times you don't obey him is, if it violates Scripture or your conscience. But other than that, in all opinion areas, you obey. Amen?...when he assigns you to a House church, when he assigns you to a Zone, when he assigns you to a Bible Talk, you will go, because that's part of the plan. Amen?..." [1]

#2 Hold onto a false basis of authority

"You would think these...leaders were Moses, the way they keep making up so many laws!... they love to sit at the head table... they enjoy the deference paid them on the streets, and to be called 'Rabbi,' and 'Master!' Don't let anyone call you that. For only God is your Rabbi and all of you are on the same level, as brothers." Matt 23: 1, 6-9 LB

In the Boston Movement, as stated earlier, Kip McKean is considered the "top dog." He acknowledged in his sermon, "The Super Church" at the World Missions Leadership Conference that a hierarchy exists with himself at the top. [2] In the September 4, 1988 issue of the *Boston Bulletin*, McKean stated,

"...Her leadership (speaking of Pat Gempel, an elder's wife and woman's counselor, SM) of all the women in the movement, her incredible creativity and her problem-solving techniques have, more than any other person, shaped *my decisions for the Boston church and the entire Multiplying Ministry Movement...*" (italics mine, SM) [3]

McKean rules the ongoings of the Movement and orders who should step down and who should take over. No one goes or does anything without his approval. He is considered above the elders (all evangelists in the Movement are) and has the responsibility of discipling them. Even after moving out of Boston, Al Baird (one of the Boston elders) stated "Kip will continue to disciple the Boston elders and return to Boston from time to time just as Paul did in Ephesus."[4] McKean also appointed his successors as lead evangelist at the Boston Church of Christ. (First, Tom Brown, then Al Baird, then Randy McKean.)

McKean likens his plan for evangelizing the world to the way "God laid on the heart of Nehemiah a plan to rebuild Jerusalem." He said at the 1988 Denver Reconstruction:

"...somebody has got to have the plan. I don't claim to be any kind of apostle, prophet or anything like that, but I believe with all of my heart a few years ago the Lord put that plan upon my heart. And *you cannot have qualms about me...* I am not perfect. But *you cannot have any bad attitudes toward me personally or toward the Boston church...*"[5] (italics mine, SM)

Although McKean states he is not an apostle, he is, according to God, to "follow the pattern of Paul's role in the first century."[6] And nobody is *allowed* to doubt that! He believes he and the evangelists he appoints are "anointed" of God just like David, Jeremiah, or Moses and "God's people must be aware that they have a responsibility before God to respect, obey, and submit to His anointed servants."[7]

McKean acts and is revered as if he were indeed the Apostle Paul. No one else is on his level. Sam Laing, who was the campus minister at Gainesville when Kip was converted and later retrained under Kip in Boston, said, "...Kip McKean is the greatest living treasure that God has given the kingdom on the face of the earth today..." This is a common view of those under McKean. His followers "want to be exactly like Kip" — "to preach like him... to think like him... to talk like him." They consider him the ultimate example in all areas of life — as a minister, a Christian, an evangelist, a leader, a discipler, a father, a husband and a friend.[8]

McKean points to the Movement's growing numbers as the evidence that God has raised him up for this leadership position. In his article, "Revolution Through Restoration," he states: "My challenge to all of the critics in the Churches of Christ has been — where are the souls you are saving and where are the churches you have built? We do believe 'by their fruit' (or lack of fruit) you will recognize them."[9] McKean believes what he does is God's will for everyone else — that is, if they *really* want to follow God. Leadership throughout the Boston churches follow the same line of reasoning.

Because of their success, they mistake their methods and their positions as being approved of and appointed by God. Their "authority" is based on numbers and each other, not on servant leadership or the truths of the Bible. If brother John converts X number of people and the top leader (usually meaning Kip McKean) approves of him, then it is said that "God raised him up to lead such-and-such place." The people are told to follow him without question because he is "of God." The leaders set down the rules and demand absolute obedience, trust and loyalty from the members. "Do what I say because I am the evangelist, the director, the teacher, the elder, the zone leader, or the discipler," is the general thinking. Nothing else matters. If someone gets hurt, it's because he is "too soft and sentimental and needs to buckle up." Rarely, if ever, are the leaders or their methods considered any part of the problem; it's always due to someone else's bad attitude or untrusting heart.

In the 1987 Boston Seminar, Kip McKean said:

> "The evangelist without elders in the congregation is the authority of God in the congregation. The only time he is not to be obeyed is when he calls you to disobey Scripture or disobey your conscience and even if he calls you to do something that disobeys your conscience, you still have an obligation to study it out and prayerfully *change your opinion* so you can be totally unified."[10] (italics mine, SM).

Questioning the leader is treated as questioning God. It's not allowed. The leader knows God's heart and mind better than anyone else, so the flock must think and believe like the leader. If someone tries to question or challenge them in any way, he is accused of being independent, rebellious and divisive. If he persists in the challenge of doctrine or practices, he will be asked to leave and will be marked as a troublemaker.

Boston leadership often quotes Heb. 13:17 "Obey your leaders and submit to their authority... Obey them so that their work will be a joy, not a burden..." They remind the followers to not be like Korah, who rebelled against Moses (Num 16) and was swallowed up by the earth; or like Miriam, who criticized Moses because of his wife (Num 12) and was struck temporarily with leprosy. They refer to 1 Sam 24:5-6 when David refused to kill King Saul at the urging of his friends and replied, "The Lord forbid that I should do such a thing to my master, the Lord's anointed, or lift my hand against him; for he is the anointed of the Lord."

Passages like these are used out of context to shift the focus onto the other person as the problem, to prohibit people from thinking for themselves, and to keep the leader from being held accountable. The message is "I am untouchable; God put me over you and I know better than you what you need to do. You just need to trust and follow me because God is in control."

#3 Stresses submission to a discipler

"...Among the heathen, kings are tyrants and each minor official lords it over those beneath him..." (Matt 20:25 LB) "...In this world the kings and great men order their slaves around and the slaves have no choice but to like it! But among you the one who serves you best will be your leader..." Luke 22:25-26 LB

In the Boston churches, discipleship is a requirement for baptism and membership candidates. It is not an option for any one at any age. Each person, and certainly every leader, is expected to be under a discipler for as long as they live. They are taught:

> "...A disciple is someone who understands that he is going to be discipled by man. That is God's will, it is his purpose, it is his plan and it is the only way that it makes your heart fully submissive to him when you are discipled by another person — every single person... There is no other way to be in a right relationship with God."[11]

However, Boston's concept of the discipling relationship is one *over* one, not one *to* one as the Scriptures teach. There is no equal partnership. The disciple is required to confess all sin, seek counsel on every matter, and imitate the discipler in all things — including matters of opinion. The discipler's job is to make sure he does it.

The entire focus is the disciple's obedience to the discipler, regardless if the counsel is wrong, abusive or understood. The disciple is taught that God demands submission, even in the face of abuse or error. Boston says because

Jesus submitted to abusive men at His trial and crucifixion, a disciple should follow His example and submit or risk putting himself out from under God's protection. (This is taken out of context; Jesus submitted to God, not to man and He submitted to man's *needs*, not his abuses.) God's protective covering is considered to be in the authority of the government over its people, parents over children, masters over slaves, husbands over wives, and spiritual leaders over Christians, or discipler over disciple. This last relationship is based on God discipling Jesus and Jesus discipling the twelve apostles.

The disciple is held accountable to the discipler for every area of life. (Several ministries developed "accountability sheets" to use in discipling relationships.) The discipler could dictate what to wear, how long to sleep, where to work, what personality traits need to be developed or dropped, who to date, what to believe, who to be friends with, where to vacation, how to spend money and so on. "Follow me" (read that, "Be me") is the theme of discipleship and it is thoroughly ingrained within every believer as the will and eternal plan of God for all people.

Trust is demanded from the disciple but not earned by the discipler. Disciples are taught they have no rights except to deny themselves and put the kingdom first. Their responsibility is to imitate the discipler because everything the discipler does or says is for the good of the disciple and he knows more than the disciple. They are constantly told "an awesome disciple is one who assumes his discipler is more objective and accurate about his life than he is."[12] If the disciple balks at any point, he will be told he needs to have the "open, teachable heart of a disciple." He must learn to trust because God placed him under the discipler's care and not submitting to the discipler is really not submitting to God.

Theresa Ferguason wrote in the *Boston Bulletin*:

"Also, we need to trust in God, completely to enable us to grow and, most importantly, we need to trust the people he has put in our life to help us change. Ultimately, if we do not trust these people, we do not trust God. To the extent that I trust my discipler, Gloria Baird, I am in reality trusting God."[13]

One of Kip McKean's disciples, Marty Fuqua stated, "Take authority out of discipling relationships and you have nothing."[14] It is true; without stressing submission, Boston's dictatorial management style would be impossible to maintain. The two go hand in hand. Her people allow it because they are taught and believe it is the way God intended it to be. No one wants to be found fighting against God's plan for them. The "R" word — rebellion — is the "Scarlet Letter" every disciple fears wearing.

#4 Legalistic and performance — oriented

"...They load you with impossible demands that they themselves don't even try to keep... you tithe down to the last mint leaf in your garden, but ignore the important things — justice and mercy and faith. Yes, you should tithe, but you shouldn't leave the more important things undone." Matt 23:4, 23-24 LB

Legalism produces an all-or-nothing mentality; issues are black or white with no gray areas. Either one is spiritual, by evidence of external measures, or one is not. Checklists and rule-keeping are the barometers of spiritual health: Did you share your faith today? Did you have a Quiet Time? Have you talked with your disciple? How are you showing gratitude for your discipler? Who are you studying the Bible with? Did you pray with your spouse? Are you doing weekly family devotionals? Positive answers point toward spiritual maturity and negative answers toward spiritual weakness. The use of such checklists or accountability sheets, it is believed, will lead to a disciplined life and make one pleasing to God. On the other hand, failure to maintain the spiritual disciplines displeases God. It shows one is unworthy of his calling.

It operates on a daily basis like this: A "strong" Christian gets up early to have a "Quiet Time" (devotional and prayer time); studies the Bible with a non-Christian; encourages a fellow Christian; and takes direction from his discipler. Here the Christian feels God is pleased and loves him. His relationship with God feels strong and he thinks he is growing strong in the faith. A "weak" Christian oversleeps or otherwise gets up too late for his morning "Quiet Time;" shows up for the Bible study but the non-Christian doesn't; forgets to make the call or write the card to encourage the other Christian and doesn't "check in" with his discipler about the day's activities. Here the Christian feels (or is told) God is angry and does not accept him until he repents and "gets it right." He tells himself he shouldn't have been so lazy; he should have reminded the non-Christian again about the study; he should have prayed more; and he should have written the card before bedtime.

Although God's love is not conditioned on our performance, it is presented as if it is. In Boston, having a regular "Quiet Time;" sharing one's faith daily; and following the lead of the disciple indicates a spiritual and faithful person. Struggling in any of these three areas would make one's relationship to God and commitment level suspect. For example, if a church converted 100 people last year and only 100 this year, they would be considered "weak," or "lazy." They would be told God is sick of their complacency and they need to repent and go back to their first love. All this just because the numbers weren't higher than the year before! (Boston would have trouble with the Old Testament prophets like Isaiah, Jeremiah, or Elijah; throughout their combined ministries, very few people turned to God.)

The rule keeping isn't limited to a written code of conduct or a "to do" list. Most of it exists in the form of "hidden rules," like "Quiet Times" should be at least an hour long and first thing in the morning. These rules are discovered only by breaking them and/or being pressured to fit into a certain mold.

A little rule keeping, however, leads to bigger rule keeping. And rule keeping leads to requirements God never intended. For instance, Boston teaches discipleship must begin before baptism, not afterwards, based on the Great Commission: "Therefore go and make disciples of all nations, baptizing them in the name of the Father, the Son and the Holy Spirit." (Matt 28:19). An element of truth does exist in this teaching in that one must understand what the Christian life is about and then make a decision to follow the truths of the Bible, but it is taken to an extreme. Boston adds requirements for becoming a Christian that are un-biblical. For example, in the Boston churches no one is baptized unless he is already sharing his faith, attending all the services, speaking up in class and agrees to being under a discipler. (This is how they know if one is a disciple.) If he does not agree to discipling, he is told he does not have a discipler's heart and is not ready for baptism. (This reminds me of Jesus' words to the Pharisees: "...you shut the kingdom of heaven in men's faces... you won't let those enter who are trying to..." Matt 23:13)

It goes even further; anyone who did not believe this way at the time of baptism is not considered a Christian. Nor is anyone who answers these questions in the negative: Were you cut to the heart by the cross before you were baptized? Did you confess and repent of all sin in your life? Were you a committed disciple before you were baptized? Did you understand and crucify your sinful nature before baptism? Did you respond to Christ or merely flee from God's wrath? Were you converted to Jesus or to the right church, the right doctrine, the right baptism? Did you understand you were saved at the point of baptism? (These questions are asked of everyone in the "reconstruction" of a church and of those who wish to train under Boston.) Any uncertainty leads to the conclusion of an invalid baptism. This person must be rebaptized or he will remain lost.

Elena McKean (Kip's wife) sums up Boston's concept of who is "saved" in her article in the December 20, 1987 issue of the *Boston Bulletin*: "...Only baptized disciples will be willing to go anywhere, do anything, and give up everything for the cause of winning the world..."[15] The inference is that if one is not willing to do any of these things, then one is not a disciple and is not saved. Kip McKean echoes the same in his article, "Revolution Through Restoration": "When one is born again at baptism, one must have Jesus' heart and attitude — do anything, go anywhere and give up everything for God."[16] If a member does not wish to go where Boston chooses to send him, his being a disciple, that is being saved, is questioned since a "true disciple" would have no qualms of where or what God calls him to do.

All these extra rules and requirements result in either smug or burdened people. The smug people usually take on leadership roles and the burdened ones drop out or keep a low profile. Their talk gives them away. The speeches and conversations are peppered with terminology like: "I really need to change in this area," "Christians should do this or be like that," and "I just gotta die to self." They speak of being "*totally* committed," "*totally* open," and "*totally* submissive." During the response time, individuals ask for forgiveness for "being a lousy disciple," and request prayers to have hearts that are "pure and committed to God in being obedient disciples," to be a person "of conviction;" to "dream bigger dreams;" "to open his heart to his discipler;" to not allow himself to "limit God's work;" and to "have a heart like his discipler."

#5 Image-conscious

"You are so careful to polish the outside of the cup, but the inside is foul with extortion and greed... First cleanse the inside of the cup, and then the whole cup will be clean... you are like beautiful mausoleums — full of dead men's bones, and of foulness and corruption. You try to look like saintly men, but underneath those pious robes of yours are hearts besmirched with every sort of hypocrisy and sin." Matt 23: 25-28 LB

The services at the Boston churches are exciting but a closer examination shows the church is not what she appears to be. Those training for leadership roles are told to publicly praise their discipler every time they speak. Leaders especially favored by Kip McKean are given "zones" padded with the most fruitful members so they could "be raised up." The unconditional love so often preached about is conditioned on one's obedience to the leaders. They talk of unity, but they practice uniformity by concentrating on keeping the external rules of measurement and productivity. Everyone must believe and act exactly the same on every subject. There is no room for opinions, individualism, or questions.

The blueprint for shaping one into "Christlikeness" is based on the style and personality of the leader. That one style or personality is the only one held up as being useful for the Kingdom. Members are molded into this image without regard for the individual's talents, skills, or personality. This molding is confused as "spiritual growth." Acting, talking, thinking, and sounding like one's discipler is thought to be the mark of maturity.

Discipleship partners are often mismatched because the "goal" (of forming the "image") is more important than the needs of the individual. For instance, a middle-aged man who is married and has a household of teenagers might be assigned to be discipled by a single or newly married younger man. The older man is expected to follow the direction of the younger man in terms of his ministry, his family, and his marriage. The young discipler is given this authority, not because of his proven wisdom and experience, but because he matches the image the Movement wishes to foster as being a "dedicated, serving disciple."

In maintaining the image, members are admonished to be "all things to all people." No one should know more about love, joy, peace, or fun than Christians because they know God. "So show it!" they are told; be the best for the "honor of God's name." Be the best worker, the best student, the best dressed, the most out-going, the most fun-loving, the most confident, the most fit, the most serving and so on. To do less will dishonor Him.

This leads to double messages. It's the "catch-22" where no matter what one does, it's either wrong or not enough. As students we were told to get the best grades, but if we were found with blocks of time devoted to studying, we were reprimanded for being tied to the world. We were told to "seek the kingdom first" by doing the Lord's work first in order to honor Him. Then, when we didn't receive good grades, we were reproved for bringing dishonor to the Kingdom and not attracting the world to God. Likewise, if family problems arose because the father or mother were neglecting the children for church work, the parents were reminded of their responsibility to first "rule their own house well." But if a church program or Bible study conflicted with the needs of the family, they were told "whoever loves mother, father, brother, sister, child... more than me is not worthy of me."

#6 Kill their wounded

"Beware of false teachers who come disguised as harmless sheep, but are wolves and will tear you apart. You can detect them by the way they act, just as you can identify a tree by its fruit." Matt 7:15 LB

Focusing so much energy on maintaining an image leads to not allowing any perceived weaknesses. Real problems are not discussed unless one is winning, or has won over them. The typical answer given to someone with a problem is to forget about yourself and just concentrate on saving the lost and serving the brotherhood. Jesus made us all new creatures and wiped out our pasts, so get over it and forget it; don't hold onto it. If one continues to struggle, he is of weak character, lazy, and double-minded. He will be shunned and reminded that "all liars and cowards will be thrown into the lake of fire."

A "no-talk" rule prevails within the Movement. Wanting to discuss a hurtful incident is considered as living in the past or being divisive and self-centered. The member is told to "die to self and put the past in the past." Don't talk about it anymore. If one is hurt by someone in the church, he is told he just needs to accept the truth in whatever way it was offered, make the necessary changes, and above all else, drop his pride and forgive and forget. If someone leaves the fellowship, no one is told the real reason; the leaders just say that person had "sin in his heart and is a warning for the rest of us to pursue godliness."

If someone questions a decision, a method, a teaching or a policy, he is attacked for being prideful and rebellious. (Any criticism or independence is called "sin.") He is told he has a bad attitude or a bad heart and needs to repent. His loyalty and spirituality is questioned. Everything is turned around so that he is the problem, not whatever the real issue is. If he holds a leadership position, it might be taken away and future ones withheld until he proves to be "repentant and committed." The environment is "don't ask, don't talk."

If someone continues to question or is critical of the Movement or her leaders, especially Kip McKean, he is considered disloyal and is publicly marked at a church meeting to not be associated with by the other members. Absolutely no contact can happen. No coffee talks, no "hello, how are you" chance meetings at the mall, no nothing. It is as if he is dead. If someone does converse with him, he will be marked as well.

At the San Diego Missions Conference, Tom Brown stated "The biggest tradition and sin of all is accepting lukewarm members."[17] And at a Bible Study Leaders' Workshop conducted by Kip McKean and Al Baird in Atlanta, all the participants were told to "get with the program or get out." They could decide to hold themselves and those in their study to the commitment outlined in the workshop, or they could leave. They were given a form to indicate their decision and told to choose within the next couple of weeks.[18]

Boston's attitude towards the "weaker" members is summed up in one leader's comments to his group: "I'm not interested in meeting your needs... The kingdom is not a hospital for the wounded people; it's an army of soldiers — soldiers who are strong in the grace of God, soldiers who are doing God's will..."[19]

#7 Elitism

" '...Beware of the yeast of the Pharisees and Sadducees'... then at last they understood that by 'yeast' he meant the wrong teaching of the Pharisees and Sadducees..." (Matt 16: 6,16 LB) "...false teachers, like vicious wolves, will appear among you, not sparing the flock. Some of you yourselves will distort the truth in order to draw a following..." Acts 20:29,30 LB

Boston considers herself to have the corner on the truth and the responsibility to convert everyone else to her way of believing since she is the only church to teach the concept of "baptize only disciples." Believing only she is the true "Remnant," she continues to call everyone who is "committed" to join her. Those in her own fellowship who do not agree with all that she does are thought of as "unspiritual" and "unwilling to pay the cost of following Jesus." They are usually asked and encouraged to leave.

This "elite" outlook ("We're right and everyone else is wrong") shows in Kip McKean's speech at the World Missions Leadership Conference in July, 1992. At the time, McKean was discussing the reconstruction of the Orlando church:

"Some of you guys — let me just lay it out, you flat didn't have a church of disciples until we did the ˟cotton pickin'˟ reconstruction. Now remember that and flat get grateful. You had people from mainline, you got people from campus ministry... Remember what was done. 'Now we had the church in here for eight years.' No you didn't. You had a group of some disciples and some yoyos you let in that couldn't tell the difference between the rest of you."[20]

Remember, this was said to a church who came *willingly* under Boston's control! This lack of respect is typical for reconstructed churches. "You were nothing until we got here and you should thank God eternally for us."

The churches unwilling to follow Boston's direction are more than un-respected; they are "flat out lost." Joe Garmon said at the Brockton House Church Reconstruction:

"People in the churches of Christ who have not been discipled first and then baptized are not saved... We believe those who have left here have left the church — have left the Lord. And we believe the churches of Christ in general do not teach, do not preach, do not believe in — as a matter of fact, oppose — the doctrine of making disciples before baptism. And because of that the vast majority of people in the church of Christ are not saved."[21]

#8 Stresses "total" commitment

"Not all who sound religious are really godly people. They may refer to me as 'Lord,' but still won't get to heaven. For the decisive question is whether they obey my Father in heaven. At the Judgment many will tell me, 'Lord, Lord, we told others about you and used your name to cast out demons and to do many other great miracles.' But I will reply, 'You have never been mine. Go away, for your deeds are evil.' Matt 23:21-23 LB

The Boston messages emphasize one must give up everything to follow God; there can be no room left for selfishness. The work of the kingdom demands one to give up all rights to one's time, possessions, preferences, desires, goals, relationships, energy, attitudes, thoughts, and feelings.

The problem is, "all rights" are usually given to the leaders, not to God. The leaders define what "total commitment" is — and isn't. If they feel someone should be more involved, he will be advised to quit or change jobs, take less classes, move to a place where better discipling is happening, give up a relationship or do "whatever it takes" to be committed. Those who follow the advice are publicly lifted up as examples of having "a heart for God." (Nancy once remarked she had not seen Jack, her husband, in three days!) I've known several gifted athletes and musicians who gave up full scholarships so they could "serve God only and put the kingdom first."

Turning down a leader's "request" or "advice" can lead to a "breaking" session. This could be one or a multitude of lengthy talks until the "no" becomes "yes." The person is told he needs to be "broken" over his sins of having a hard heart, not being a good disciple, and not submitting to the leadership God placed over him. He is told how much he is loved and cared for and how the discipler "just wants the best" for him. He is told about the discipler's vision for his life and how much potential he has if he would just live up to it. He is blamed for his "lack of growth" and told how it holds back his family and friends in following God. He should have been ready to take on more responsibilities already, but instead, he's still learning the fundamentals. His "complacency" is holding back the kingdom and the blessings of God because he is not mature. If he finally agrees to whatever the other wants him to do, but doesn't seem broken enough, the talks will continue. And continue. Until finally he will say or do anything to be left alone. Although there is no physical damage, this must be similar to what prisoners of war feel when they're "broken" by their enemy.

I once heard someone say that the average Boston member burns out within four years. I don't have any figures to back that up, but from what I have experienced and seen in others, it sounds pretty accurate.

#9 Stresses only evangelism as "fruit"

"... you go to all lengths to make one convert, and then turn him into twice the son of hell you are yourselves..." (Matt 23:15 LB)

The ministry is both the goal and the god of the Boston churches. The focus is on the number of conversions and "taking it higher" than before. The pressure of keeping the numbers in an upward trend has turned Boston into a "numbers cruncher." What matters is having more baptisms this year than the year before. If the numbers drop, the church is considered "another mainline church" and the members lacking in zeal.

An article by Gordon Ferguson (a Boston elder) illustrates Boston's emphasis:

"For years, I have been puzzled by 'Christians' who were resistant to sharing their faith and to doing other things taught in the New

Testament. I am no longer puzzled. Either these people **never** became disciples, or they **quit** being disciples. In either case, they are not saved. Calling ourselves 'Christians' or 'members of the church' means nothing. If we are not doing what disciples are commanded to do, **we are not saved.** And my personal conviction is that many of those in 'churches of Christ' have never biblically repented, have never become disciples, and are thus not Christians. A large number of people, including me, have faced the issue and have been baptized with a true disciple's repentance..." [22]

Before someone is baptized, he is taught to share his faith; afterwards he is pushed to "bear fruit." What he does with his time will be evaluated. *Any* activity, (exercise, sports, hobbies, grocery shopping, etc.) that is not used in an evangelistic outreach will have to change or be dropped. If he is not bringing someone to Bible Talk or to church within a certain amount of time there will be a "heart-to-heart" talk with his discipler, Bible Talk leader, house leader, or zone leader.

The majority of the sermons center on evangelism and discipleship. (A friend of mine remarked that in the whole time she heard Jack preach, she only heard one sermon — over and over again.) Developing the "fruits of the Spirit" is only discussed in connection with making disciples of the nations. As far as Boston is concerned, if one is developing the fruits listed in Gal. 5:22 (love, joy, patience, self-control, gentleness), but not converting others, then he's not growing. He's not doing the "real work" of the kingdom; he's settling for the "easy Christianity." He's probably not even saved.

Members are pushed to "do whatever it takes" to win converts and show they are "worthy of their calling." Evangelism — and the numbers to back it up — is the only proof one is truly a disciple of the Lord. It is the only work God will commend us for in Heaven. He will burn everything else. How far does this teaching go? Well, Nick Young's sermon in Tulsa is typical of Boston's emphasis on evangelistic productivity as proof of one's salvation. As a well trained disciple, he sets down rules and quotas as if they were Biblical commands and his attitude towards those not from Boston is illustrative of the Movement. Young was sent by Boston to reconstruct Tulsa in August 1992.

"...If you had a biblical conversion, you were totally fired up and totally committed and you were zealous in the Lord and you were sharing your faith with every one you met, you have a biblical conversion. You weren't doing those things. And so calling you back to your first love is irrelevant because you have never had a first love... I am totally convinced that had the mission team not come here, the group that was waiting here would all be lost. And many of you are lost right now — maybe all of you are lost — you're lost in your lukewarmness and in your sin and in your fear and in your unbelief. You're lost because of your lack of love for God. You're lost in your rebelliousness to God... this mission planting, first of all is to help you get saved. And once we get you saved, then we can save this city... You are going to go out with the gospel of Jesus, and you're not going to have a problem with inviting 30 a day... I have heard that some of you have actually had an attitude about having to share with 30 people a day. That makes me sick! And it makes God sicker! Where is your heart? Have you lost your faith? You've lost your heart. You can't even take a simple challenge like sharing with 30 people a day and not get all bent out of shape about it. Do you see why the church planting has come? It has come for your sake. You're the lost. You're the one that needs to be saved. You're the one that is going to go to hell if you don't repent. You need to be the most grateful person in this entire city because you were hell bound before this planting came... You're repenting now and hopefully you can be saved..."[23]

The number or the rule might change from church to church, but this type of demand, manipulation, and shaming technique is common from the leadership within the Boston Movement.

#10 Often lack formal training in theology and/or counseling

"...Your error is caused by your ignorance of the Scriptures and of God's power... Don't you ever read the Scriptures?" Matt 22: 29,31 LB

Education and degrees are not a requirement to become a minister or a women's counselor. Since Christian schools do not teach baptism and discipleship the way Boston does, they are not believed helpful in any other theological matter. Learning psychology and counseling techniques are brushed off because the world does not teach about "dealing with sin." The only requirement for leadership position is to "bear fruit." Evangelism and discipleship is where the Holy Spirit and the Bible would teach one everything necessary to know in leading others.

Training begins with walking daily with one's discipler. The discipler would teach, correct, direct and guide the disciple into becoming a "person of God." This is based on the 12 disciples walking with Jesus on a daily basis. Boston points out that the Twelve did not go off to a seminary or graduate school; they lived with Jesus from day to day and He trained them.

What she doesn't point out is that *was* the normal way all the rabbi's of Jesus' day taught their students! That *was* "seminary!"

I'm not saying education is a fail-safe; there are some highly educated ministers who lack spirituality and harm the Body of Christ too. In fact the verses quoted above were spoken by Jesus to some of the most highly educated men in His time! These men could quote the Old Testament and probably every commentator as well, but Jesus said they didn't really know the Scriptures. Neither extreme, all school or no school but God, is sufficient. But proper training combined with a strong relationship with God can make the difference in being able to effectively lead people in positive, healthy directions. To put someone over a group of people without the necessary tools and ability to minister is dangerous. Often it is the "worldly" counselors called upon to undo the damage wrought by the "godly" counselors!

#11 Wear "persecution" as a seal of approval from God

"How often I have wanted to gather your children together as a hen gathers her chicks beneath her wings, but you wouldn't let me..." Matt 23: 38 LB

Criticism is not tolerated or given any thought to how true it might be. All criticism is called "sin." Members are told persecution always comes to the godly and they need to keep focused on God's work. Satan is attacking them because they are the "Remnant."

Kip McKean refers to criticism as "spiritual pornography." Members are told not to read the articles, the letters, or the books that expose them, nor watch the programs that denounce them. They are warned (threatened is a better term) not to talk to former members. Instead, they are encouraged to be like Nehemiah and not allow the distractions of those who are against the "Lord's work" to stop them from their "mission." Criticism and fallaways have not caused Boston to reconsider her actions; she just closes the ranks and keeps going.

#12 Difficult to leave

Leaving the Boston Movement is more than walking out the door. It is probably the hardest decision one will make. The conditioning one has been subjected to breaks down the will, the ability to think clearly, and the strength to make unpopular, albeit healthy, decisions. Most members only know other members — these are the only ones they are allowed to live with, date, marry and sometimes work with. Walking away is leaving everyone they know and everything they once believed and stood for publicly.

At first, many will come after the "erring one" in efforts to win him back into the fold. If he can withstand the threats, the emotional blackmail, the manipulation, and the dismal pictures painted of himself, Boston will mark him and no one will ever talk to him again. Ever. It can be very lonely.

On top of that, ex-members are filled with guilt and wonder if they are leaving the true church and entering the road to Hell. The services were uplifting and the leaders were charismatic and persuasive speakers; they appeared to know all the answers and have life all wrapped up. They remember the good times they had and the promises of the leaders to change some of the erroneous teachings. Did they make a mistake in leaving? Should they have stayed and tried to work it out? Are they crucifying Jesus again as they were told they are? Will they fall back into their old sins? Will God have anything to do with them? Does God even care about what has happened? If the ex-member cannot find a strong church again, these self-doubts and questions magnify.

---

[1]   Jerry Jones' *WDTBMT?* Vol. 1, p. 9

[2]   Jerry Jones' *WDTBMT?* Vol. 3, p. 22

[3]   Reprinted in Jerry Jones' *WDTBMT?* Vol. 1, p. 113

[4]   *Boston Bulletin,* reprinted in Jerry Jones' *WDTBMT?* Vol. 2, p. 77

[5]   Jerry Jones' *WDTBMT?* Vol. 1, p. 40

[6]   *Boston Bulletin,* June 26, 1988; reprinted in Jerry Jones' *WDTBMT?* Vol. 1, p. 106

[7]   Jerry Jones' *WDTBMT?* Vol. 1, pp. 38-44; Vol. 2, p. 12; Vol. 3, pp. 17-19; 27-29

[8]   Jerry Jones' *WDTBMT?* Vol. 1, pp. 38-39

[9]   Jerry Jones' *WDTBMT?* Vol. 3, p. 110

[10]   Jerry Jones' *WDTBMT?* Vol. 1, p. 9

[11]   Joe Garmon quote; reprinted in Jerry Jones' *WDTBMT?* Vol. 1, p. 18

[12]   *Chicago Fire,* "How To Be An Awesome Disciple," reprinted in Jerry Jones' *WDTBMT?* Vol. 1, p. 114

[13]   *Boston Bulletin,* "Forever Growing," Jerry Jones' *WDTBMT?* Vol. 1, pp. 11, 77

[14]   Jerry Jones' *WDTBMT?* Vol. 3, p. 23

[15]   Jerry Jones' *WDTBMT?* Vol. 1, p. 26

[16]   Jerry Jones' *WDTBMT?* Vol. 3, p. 106

[17]   Jerry Jones' *WDTBMT?* Vol. 1, p. 31

[18]   Jerry Jones' *WDTBMT?* Vol. 1, pp. 35, 132

[19]   Jerry Jones' *WDTBMT?* Vol. 2, p. 51

[20]   Jerry Jones' *WDTBMT?* Vol. 3, p. 42

[21]   Jerry Jones' *WDTBMT?* Vol. 1, p. 28

[22]   "Progressive Revelation, Part IV: Disciple's Baptism," *Boston Bulletin,* reprinted in Jerry Jones' *WDTBMT?* Vol. 1, pp. 27, 75

[23]   Jerry Jones' *WDTBMT?* Vol. 3, pp. 24, 42

What Makes the Movement Dangerous

"...Woe to the shepherds who feed themselves instead of their flocks. Shouldn't shepherds feed the sheep? You eat the best food and wear the finest clothes, but you let your flocks starve. You haven't taken care of the weak nor tended the sick nor bound up the broken bones nor gone looking for those who have wandered away and are lost. Instead you have ruled them with force and cruelty. So they were scattered, without a shepherd. They have become a prey to every animal that comes along. My sheep wandered through the mountains and hills and over the face of the earth, and there was no one to search for them or care about them..." Ezekiel 34: 2-6 LB

Not everything about the Boston Movement is bad. If it were *all* bad, leaving would not present such a problem. In fact, much of what she does is what the church *should* be doing. Boston's goals are right; spreading the gospel and making disciples through out the world was commanded by Jesus and is part of the church's purpose here on earth. The church *should* be actively converting the lost and developing the believers into maturity. Having exciting assemblies, developing strong relationships, respecting the leadership, dealing with sin, and sharing our faith is what the church is all about.

If churches do not provide this environment, cults like Boston will. Boston grows because those seeking a meaningful faith in the Lord are attracted to her "aliveness." The talk is on restoring New Testament Christianity and applying the Bible to everyday life. That's what spiritually hungry people want — an active faith, not a "spectator event."

But for all of Boston's good, she has done more in damaging people than in saving them. In her desire to develop a "faithful remnant," she has become a spiritually abusive organization. Although her goal to follow the Great Commission is right, how she tries to fulfill that command, i.e., by "doing whatever it takes to get the job done," has opened the door to abuse. The end justifies the means, no matter who gets hurt in the process. The real needs of the flock (encouragement, patience, support, etc.) are generally discounted in favor of attaining the goal (converts). It's spiritual cannibalism.

What makes the Boston Movement dangerous is her abusiveness. The last chapter gave several examples of this. She does not allow her people to make mistakes or even simple choices about their lives. She does not provide an environment where problems can be openly discussed and solved. Her members do not have freedom of expression, nor can they "be their own person." She tells them what to believe, what to think, who to follow, and what to become. She determines one's spiritual standing and worth before God by his number of converts or amount of prayer time. She demands her people jump through religious hoops to prove themselves and punishes them when they can't. She shames them into repentance and compliance to her standards and calls it God's eternal plan. In a different context, this would, without a doubt, be called abuse.

The Boston Movement did not start out the way she is now. Her views prior to 1986 on authority, autonomy of the churches, baptism, and discipleship are not the views she currently holds. (Jerry Jones traces the changes in these views from Boston's own material, particularly in the second volume of *What Does the Boston Movement Teach?*)

Boston's phenomenal success and vow to "take it higher" has caused her to focus on herself instead of looking at Christ. As a result, she has departed from the very Scriptures she professes to be "restoring." Her "do whatever it takes to make it work" philosophy has built an hierarchy and a narrow, legalistic theology she viciously protects. Her loyalty has turned towards her leaders and away from the Bible. The "Movement" has taken over the place of God.

The main lesson I've learned from my time in the Boston Movement is this: just because it says "God" does not make it "godly." Likewise, just because one is following a God-given command does not make the method right. The end does not justify the means.

In our society we often hear about abuse. For instance, when someone drinks in response to problems, we call it alcohol abuse. When a husband beats his wife, we call it spousal abuse; when a parent calls a child degrading names, we call it emotional abuse, but when a church leader demands unquestioning obedience and blind loyalty, Boston calls it God's Will.

Or is it spiritual abuse?

Understanding some of the dynamics of spiritual abuse was the first step on the road to freedom and faith for me. It helped me sort through and make sense of my experiences and my role in the Boston ministry. I'd like to share some of these thoughts with you.

What spiritual abuse is and who does it

In his book, *Healing Spiritual Abuse*, Ken Blue says "...spiritual abuse happens when a leader with spiritual authority uses that authority to coerce, control or exploit a follower, thus causing spiritual wounds."[1] This is an excellent definition of abuse as well as an accurate description of the dynamics in the Boston Movement.

This is how it works: one person, the "abusee," looks to the other person, the "abuser," to "lead" him in spiritual development. This "leader" might hold a title, such as minister, or might be the one who led him to Christ. However, it's important to understand that "leadership" is not limited to a title or office like, pastor, elder or deacon. *Leadership includes anyone who is looked up to by another in order to grow.* Regardless if the abuser has a title or not, he is perceived by both parties as having some type of authority over the other. In Boston, the disciplers, Bible Talk leaders, house leaders, and zone leaders have authority over everyone in their charge.

The abusers, however, have their own hidden agenda. They use the sheep to fulfill their own personal needs or professional goals. They're not really concerned about helping the weak, or the sick, or the injured. They want sheep that reflect well on themselves as leaders. They see the sheep as notches on their Bibles, as future Bible Talk leaders, zone leaders, financial supporters of church plantings, or missionaries. Their concern is in gratifying their needs of value, worth, importance, respect, and power. They do this through the well tuned performance of those under their "care."

Abusers demand a certain level of "spirituality" from the followers based on externals, like attendance, appearance, amount of prayer time, Bible studies, and the number of visitors brought to services. They judge the disciples as "weak," "uncommitted," "lazy," or "ungrateful" if they fail to reach the desired level.

They use their authority to intimidate and dominate the ones looking to them for guidance. ("Listen to me because I'm your discipler.") They use Scripture wrongfully to back up what they want done. ("Joe evangelist is anointed of God just like Moses or Jeremiah and you must obey him in all things.") They teach a view of God that is really an image of themselves. ("The lack of conversions shows your lukewarmness and it makes God nauseous.") In reality, they crave power (over others) to fill their own inner voids.

Christian ministry and leadership roles often attract people who want to help others but also have serious needs of their own. They may harbor a deep sense of insecurity, insignificance, and weakness. They compensate for these feelings and their fear of failure by controlling others. They are more heavy-handed in their approach (than secure leaders), especially if they feel threatened, because they desire a safe, predictable environment in which they "matter." They may misuse power as a form of strength and self-defense, particularly if they have hurts carried over from the past. They manipulate and control as a way to feel accepted, valued, and important. They want to "be somebody."

Abusers sometimes see, or dream of, themselves as "heroes." They may be overly focused on doing some "great work for the Lord's kingdom" that has never happened before. They "bulldoze" anyone or anything that gets in their way. Failure by themselves or those who do the work is not an option. They crave the admiration and near worship of their followers. They make special claims like being the "anointed of the Lord" or talk about "the important work God gave them to do." They present themselves as knowing more about God's mind than anyone else. They make their followers feel unique by telling them how different and committed they are than other churches; they are the "faithful remnant." The abuser who is full of self-importance has the same needs as the one who feels greatly insecure: to be important, to be valued, to be respected and to "make a difference."

When abusers gain power, they will not let go. Having power over others can be like an addictive drug; each time they use it, they need more the next time to feel the same "high." As abusers climb the ladder of power and position, they surround themselves with those who admire them, think like them, support them, and ignore their faults. They build a hierarchical structure with only themselves at the top, those like them in the middle, and those they feel threatened by at the bottom. They place demands on people and tell them it is the only way to please God. They are obsessed with the need to control the lives of others so they feel successful. ("This church was lost until we got here.") It's easier to demand others be in a discipling relationship and threaten them with Hell if they're not, than it is to let them make that decision. Creating uniformity is always easier than creating unity. But it is not the same, except to an abuser.

Unfortunately, this is the secret behind the "success" of the Boston Movement.

Abuse and Authority

Remember, in abusive religious organizations or relationships, three things happen: (1) God is misrepresented, usually by misinterpreting Scripture, taking a passage out of context, creating false demands (where

God has not), or emphasizing a Biblical truth to an extreme; (2) people are used to fulfill the abusers needs or goals; and (3) the result is damaging to one's faith and/or person. The one seeking help is left weakened and confused, instead of being strengthened and encouraged.

As told in the second chapter, the time I asked Nancy (the women's counselor for the campus ministry) to be relieved of teaching the weekly dormitory Bible Talks is a good illustration of the above dynamics. She did not listen to the time constraints I had with my jobs and schoolwork. Nor did she offer any help or advice on time management or study habits. Instead, she made it a spiritual problem by saying my lack of faith was the issue, not my lack of time. She called into question my relationship with God and I listened because she was the "leader" and I thought she knew more than I did. I gave her the power to abuse. Although I will never know the true motive behind her "counseling," I believe it was driven by the desire for a successful campus ministry (as seen in the number of ongoing evangelistic Bible Talks). At any rate, it was not for my best interest, nor for those under me. This was one of many instances that damaged my perception of God and lowered my self-esteem.

Before we go any further, I'd like to place a "disclaimer" in here. Having a strong or aggressive personality does not mean one is abusive. Neither is talking to someone about sin in his life or upholding certain standards, like proper dress or conduct. Desiring a successful ministry is not abusive. Making mistakes is not abusive. Abuse is using external measures to determine one's spiritual worth. Abuse is making others feel second rate because they're not like someone else. Abuse is using God to say things God did not say in order to manipulate others into fulfilling our own needs and agenda.

A Look at True Authority

Whenever someone hesitates to follow a Boston directive, she is quick to whip out Heb. 13:17 — "Obey your leaders and submit to their authority. They keep watch over you as men who must give an account. Obey them so that their work will be a joy, not a burden, for that would be of no advantage to you." She even uses it to tell someone to sell his possessions or house in order to contribute more money to the church. (Selling one's home doesn't violate Scripture or one's conscience, so according to Boston one must submit to the leader's request or be in "rebellion to God.") Let's look at the total picture.

The New Testament word for "obey" is "peitho" and refers to the type of trust given a leader *voluntarily* because one is "persuaded" from learning truth and seeing the outcome of the leader's life and character. "Peitho" does not refer to a military type of obedience that is demanded and enforced because of someone's rank or decree. "Peitho" happens as one is *persuaded* by the truth and *chooses* to follow it. As the leaders serve well (in teaching and being examples), the people grant more and more freedom for them to lead. This is not about blind loyalty. There is no coercion, no obligation, and no heavy burdens. "Peitho" obedience is seen throughout the Scriptures.

Heb. 13:7 — "Remember your leaders, who spoke the word of God to you. *Consider the outcome of their way of life* and imitate their faith." (NIV)

1 Pet. 5:2,3 — "Be shepherds of God's flock that is under your care, serving as overseers — not because you must, but because you are willing, as God wants you to be; not greedy for money, but *eager to serve; not lording it over those entrusted to you, but being examples to the flock."* (NIV; the Living Bible phrases it as "...Feed the flock... not for what you will get out of it, but because you are eager to serve the Lord. Don't be tyrants, but lead them by your good example...")

Matt. 20:25-28 — "You know that the rulers of the Gentiles lord it over them, and their high officials exercise authority over them. *Not so with you.* Instead, whoever wants to become great among you must be your servant... *just as the Son of Man did not come to be served, but to serve,* and to give his life as a ransom for many." (NIV)

When Jesus said "The teachers of the Law and the Pharisees sit in the seat of Moses," (Matt. 23:2 NIV), he was referring to how they seized power over people's lives. "The seat of Moses" was an actual stone chair or throne placed in front of a synagogue. The Pharisees and other teachers of the law would sit in this seat and command the common people to listen and follow all their rules. They had lots of rules, too. Because they knew the law, they felt qualified to take this position themselves and demanded everyone else to obey them. Their authority was false because God did not give it to them nor did the people elect them to leadership.

However, throughout the New Testament, no one is given authority based on position or title. No one is given the power to "make" others submit and obey. Leadership is not about demanding 100% adherence to one's own words and decrees. It's never presented as a "one upmanship" or a corporate ladder to be climbed.

The only leadership the New Testament talks about is "servant leadership." The only authority anyone has is from speaking and living out the truths of God's Word. Leaders are called to be "examples," not "rulers." Their responsibility is to "feed the flock" not beat them or use them. Giving them the proper food — the truth of the Scriptures and helping them to understand it, is what will cause the flock to grow and mature into Christlikeness. Even so, the shepherds can only put the food on the table; they are not to shove it down the sheep's throat. Sheep have to make the choice to eat.

Even Jesus, the only One who has every right to demand submission, did not use his authority the way Boston leaders do. His disciples never understood His purpose until after the resurrection, but He didn't say, "Well, your fighting about being the greatest in the kingdom and lack of understanding why I have to die proves you never became disciples in the first place. You need to count the cost and be rebaptized or you'll go to hell." What He focused on was showing them the Father and being faithful in His own life. The disciples eventually understood and gave "peitho" obedience; they trusted Jesus because of His teachings and his life. Demanding submission is "quicker," but "peitho" obedience is truer.

Jesus describes Himself as the one who "stands at the door and knocks. If anyone hears my voice and opens the door, I will come in and eat with him, and he with me." (Rev. 3:20 NIV) Jesus knocks, but He doesn't ram the door down; He leaves the opening of the door to us. He wants followers by choice, not pressure.

When Paul wrote about his own authority as an apostle, he described it as "...the authority the Lord gave us for building you up rather than pulling you down." (2 Cor. 10:8 NIV; the Living Bible says "authority to help you, not to hurt you...") He spoke of power as only being the authority to build, not to dominate.

Paul's authority to "build up" shows in the way he helped the Corinthian church grow. They were having severe problems in dealing with sin, getting along with each other, and breaking up into various factions. Notice he didn't do what Boston might have done. He didn't send in a team to reconstruct the church. He didn't tell them to be rebaptized as disciples or get out. He didn't give them quotas and, or tell them they could only date on Saturday nights from 6 p.m. to midnight. He didn't degrade them as "lousy disciples."

Instead, he loved them enough to explain the truth to them in a way they could best understand and apply it to their lives. He met the people where they were at and helped them onto maturity. He helped them see their sins without "whitewashing" them or condemning them. He never demanded submission, but he "persuaded" them to follow truth. If you read both his letters to the Corinthians, you can see how much he really cares for them as children of God, not as trophies of his ministry. It was to the Corinthian church that Paul penned the chapter on "love" (1 Cor. 13). He says in verse 3, "If I gave everything I have to poor people and if I were burned alive for preaching the Gospel but didn't love others, it would be of no value whatsoever." (LB) Here's the "Meyers" paraphrase: "If I sold all my possessions and put the money in a 'love offering' and concentrated on evangelizing the world so much that it cost me my life, but didn't really care for those I converted, it would be worthless." Paul's focus was on loving the church and serving her needs, not having her serve him.

I'd like to give you one more illustration of Biblical authority. In the second chapter of Galatians, Paul confronts Peter with his double-standard in the way he treated the Gentiles whenever Jews were around. Paul had the "authority" to confront Peter because he was "not acting in line with the truth of the gospel" (Gal. 2:14) and others were following the same erroneous example. According to Boston's system, Paul should have said nothing because Paul was spiritually younger than Peter! Paul would have been expected to submit to Peter's example even though it was wrong! They would have called Paul unsubmissive, disloyal, rebellious, prideful, independent, and divisive! Fortunately, neither Paul nor Peter had the "Bostonian" attitude because they understood truth outranks position. Authority comes from the Word of God. It is not something we take for ourselves.

The Results of Abusive Authority

Boston is abusive because she does not allow "peitho" obedience. She does not empower people in their walks with God, she disembowels them. If Joe member is shamed, belittled, degraded, or demoted because he questioned a doctrine, a method, or a policy, that is abuse. If his character and his spirituality is attacked because he drew attention to a real problem, that is abuse. Boston's environment does not allow her members to grow into the maturity God desires for His people. Instead, she clones them into the image she desires and judges their salvation by standards of productivity and not by the grace of God.

It's often said our image of God is based on the type of relationship we have with our earthly fathers. If we have a caring earthly father, we are more likely to see God as a loving Father. If our earthly father is harsh or neglectful, we transfer that same image to the Heavenly Father. There is truth to that observation, but I'd like to suggest that the concept of God is shaped more so by the life of the church, regardless of other influences. The way the church treats people is the same way people learn to view God. If the one seeking help is listened to and counseled according to his needs, then he will most likely see God as a caring Father. If, on the other hand, he is told God is not pleased unless he shares his faith with X number of people everyday, then he will see God as demanding and hard to please. This happens to ex-Boston members. The "joy of their salvation" turns into the "dread of damnation."

Every type of abuse hurts and spiritual abuse is no exception. Not only does it hurt who the person is, it undermines their understanding and re-lationship with God. After all, if you are taught, and believe, God is disgusted with you, where could you possibly go for help? It's one thing to have God on your side even if others do not care for you, but when you believe both God and man find you hard to stomach, you are left feeling worthless, helpless and hopeless.

I believe Satan, disguised as a snake in the Garden of Eden, is the father of spiritual abuse. As the scene is described in Genesis 3, we see how he misrepresents God to Eve. "Did God really say you mustn't eat from any tree in the garden?" When Eve tells him the only restriction is not to eat from the Tree of the Knowledge of Good and Evil or they will die, Satan counters with: "You will not surely die; for God knows that when you eat of it your eyes will be opened, and you will be like God, knowing good and evil." (Gen. 3:4 NIV). Satan misrepresents God by twisting His words and His plan for godliness. He manipulates her towards his desired goal, not God's. Eve considers the words of the serpent. He sounded so wise, so confident, so sincere. The fruit looked harmless and would make her godly; what could be wrong with that? After all, God did say He wanted her to become like Him. God must have sent the serpent to help her. And so Eve forgets the truth of God's Word — "Don't eat from this tree or you will die," and she reaches for the fruit. She attempted to become holy, but was separated from God instead; all because she listened to the claims of a snake.

Is it any wonder Jesus referred to abusive religious leaders as "You snakes! You brood of vipers!"? (Matt. 23:33 NIV).

Like the bad shepherds in the passage from Ezekiel, these abusers feed themselves at the expense of the sheep. They might look and act like good shepherds on the outside, but they rule with force and cruelty. They only "care" for those in their little group and leave the "undesirable" sheep (those who do not reflect well on the shepherds or hesitate to follow them) to fend for themselves. As far as the shepherds are concerned, these sheep might as well get lost because they are of "no value" in their program. The bad shepherds hold out a God who is only concerned with performance because that's what they are concerned with; it makes the shepherds look and feel good. That is, to other shepherds. As a result, the sheep "...become a prey to every animal that comes along... they wander through the mountains and hills and over the face of the earth..."

---

[1]   Ken Blue, *Healing Spiritual Abuse,* Downers Grove, IL: Intervarsity Press 1993) p. 12

The Road to Recovery

When I first left the Movement I felt a tremendous amount of freedom, like I was getting out of prison. I could finally spend my day the way I wanted to, without feeling pressured or guilty about calling someone, reading the Bible, answering to someone, or ordering my life to please others.

But, just like an ex-convict, I had a difficult time adjusting to "civilian life." I was accustomed to others telling me what to think, what to do, and what to say. Now I had to make my own decisions about my job, where to live, where to attend church, what activities to do with my friends, and how I spent my time. It was hard because I no longer had a "standard" to use as a guide; my "decision-making muscle" was weak from lack of use. I didn't trust myself to make the "right" choice.

Besides that, I was angry at God. I blamed Him for "leading" me into the Movement. I was trying to follow Him and He betrayed me. When I became a Christian, I loved God, but when I left the Movement, I was scared of Him. I thought I wanted a relationship with God, but in my heart, I believed He would only hurt me. I didn't want that anymore. I was confused about Him and confused about me. For several years I was in a "spiritual daze," so to speak. I spent eight years in the Movement and eight years getting over it. But God bought good out of both sets of years and taught me some important lessons.

One of those lessons is this: God is faithful to us. He runs to draw near to us as we draw close to Him. He doesn't force His way upon us, but He is there for us, whether we see it or not. And nothing pleases Him more than to shower His love upon us and for us to return it. He is a great God, full of mercy, truth, and love.

Leaving the Boston Movement

The way people leave the Boston Movement varies just like the reasons do. I moved to a different state; I was a "walk away." Some slip away without telling anyone. I didn't discuss or try to resolve any issues with the leadership, I just left. Other people do try to work out their differences and may end up staying (after many "breaking sessions") or may still decide to leave because they cannot uphold Boston's teachings. Others might be asked to leave. Some get fired from their full-time staff positions for being "disloyal."

One's relational ties to the Movement can make leaving difficult as well. Singles usually live together and so the "fall-away" must move out. That may present a financial obstacle. (Even more so for the paid staff member.) Leaving one's friends can be hard, but having family members who still believe in the Movement is even rougher. It puts an enormous stress on a marriage when one wants to leave and the other wants to stay. The one who wants to leave might stay because he thinks the good outweighs the bad and wants to keep his family "unified." Maybe he takes a passive role and the spouse remains active. (He however, will be treated as an outsider.). Maybe they will attend two different churches or both will leave Boston and try to find another church together. The spouse will probably still maintain contact with friends in the Boston Movement. Each scenario holds its own challenges.

Leaving the Boston Movement is a traumatic experience, much like a divorce. There may be no physical ties left after that final break, but there is plenty of baggage. As I stated in the first chapter, although I left the Movement, it didn't leave me. I had plenty of issues and "garbage" to sort through to find faith in God and peace with myself.

Everyone who leaves Boston will probably need some form of "re-habilitation." Some more extensively than others. Along with the spiritual damage they've received, there is often emotional and psychological damage as well. Ex-Boston members carry many of the same marks victims of other forms of abuse do.

My recovery time would have been much shorter had I understood the issues I had and why I had them, the reasons I was drawn to the Movement, and why I felt stuck. The next two sections may seem out of place, but they're not. Part of the recovery process is uncovering the "whys" and the "whats" of one's self so the abuse is not continued in another form at another place with another person. Recovery begins with gaining some self-knowledge.

Common Traits and Issues of Ex-Boston Members

1) *Ambivalent feelings towards God.* They may desire a relationship with God and yet have deep-seated fear and anger towards Him as well. They may try to "tread lightly" and worship at a "safe distance." They might alternate between feelings of love, fear, anger and guilt. They may ask God to help them love Him but be too intimidated to read the Bible.

2) *A false image of God.* Their image of God is very fuzzy, but what they do see is bad. In their mind they know God is loving, but in their heart He is anything but loving. They might see Him as a slave driver who's always adding to the list of demands and never satisfied with their work. Or maybe a slick businessman who attracted them by sharp advertising and when they came in, He pulled the "bait-and-switch" routine. They feel they've "been had." They may feel God holds a grudge and will set them up just to watch them fall. They might see God as military personnel who will "nail" anyone who gets out of line or fails to follow instructions. They might see Him as the one who pulled them far enough from Hell just to dangle them over its flames as a threat to keep them from "messing up." They might see God as being indifferent and not really caring about what happened to them. But worse, if they equate God with the Boston Movement, they may be so angry they will have nothing to do with Him at all.

3) *Fear of authority figures.* It can be hard to be around someone in an authority position, inside or outside the church because they feel they are being judged. They are nervous because they are waiting for the ax to fall and to be condemned. They may feel they have to have a perfect performance to please that person. They don't want to be weak or show their vulnerability because it was used against them in the past.

4) *Confuse guilt with shame.* They have an overdeveloped sense of feeling bad when they are corrected. They go past feeling the "good guilt," which helps us to correct bad behavior and move on, to internalizing it as an indictment against themselves as being defective. This deep sense of shame leads to the next characteristic:

5) *Low self-esteem.* All the negative pictures Boston drilled into their heads about who and what they are has become their own belief system to varying degrees. If they hold different opinions or feelings from those around them, they feel they must be wrong or stupid. They need the approval of others to get along in daily life or feel okay about their person. They have developed a "learned helplessness" and doubt every decision they make by themselves. They doubt anyone would like them if they "really know who I am."

6) *Don't know who they are.* In the past, others have determined who they were and how they felt; now they realize they are a stranger to themselves. They may not be able to recognize their needs. If they do, they may feel ashamed for having them. They find it hard to describe or name their feelings; they may not even be aware of them because they have denied them so long. If you ask them what their favorite food, hobby, or personal

characteristic is, they may draw a blank. They aren't familiar with who they are because they thought it was being "self-centered."

7) *Tend to be legalistic and perfectionist.* They see all of life in terms of black and white, right and wrong with no gray areas. They may try to order their life into "daily" and "weekly" activities that must be accomplished or they feel bad about themselves. For instance, the Bible must be read 7 days a week, not 5 or they aren't "trying hard enough" to know God. They are overly concerned about doing the "right thing." They agonize over every decision to be the "right" decision; they worry if they acted and talked "right" in social settings; and struggle with participating in the "right" activities. They may feel lost without having to be accountable to someone or something.

8) *Tend to be uptight and nervous.* Because they tend to be concerned about saying or doing the "right thing," they can be extremely nervous. They do not feel good about who they are and are afraid others won't like them. If people do like them, they're afraid they won't after they get to know them a little more. They have a hard time relaxing and enjoying guilt-free fun because they feel they must be "accomplishing something." Sometimes the only time they do nothing is when they are sick.

9) *Difficulty with trusting others.* Relationships are s-c-a-r-y. Because of the manipulation and emotional blackmail they experienced in the Boston Movement, they are reluctant to let anyone near them. At the same time, they want close relationships. The opposing desire for friendship and the need to protect themselves leads to a "bouncing" effect of drawing near and backing away. If they start to get close to someone, they may be happy at first, but will regret it the next morning. They are afraid the person will turn on them or misuse them. Then they back off, preparing themselves for the "big letdown," but the sense of isolation drives them back again.

10) *Difficulty with boundaries.* Since Boston does not develop healthy relationships, they may have trouble defining and respecting proper boundaries for themselves and others. They may not be sure where they end and others begin. They don't understand "personal space" as being healthy and desirable. They don't believe they should have boundaries because it's "selfish." They have trouble saying "no" (even to extremely unreasonable requests) because they don't feel they have a right to say no. They might volunteer for everything. They might buy anything a salesperson brings to their door. They might donate money to every telemarketer that calls. They have a hard time standing up to a strong willed and aggressive personality

and inwardly hate themselves for giving into them. (On the flip side, I kept such high boundaries I wouldn't let a "religious" person near me!)

11) *Tired.* Just the thought of going to church and developing Christian relationships weighs them down. Thinking about it makes them feel exhausted, due to the hectic schedule they maintained in Boston. They don't want to see another calendar or appointment book. If and when they walk through the door of the church building, they feel everyone will be tugging on their shirt sleeve to get them to attend this class, go to that meeting, or be involved in this study group.

12) *May be either over-responsible or irresponsible.* They may see themselves as needing to "fix whatever is wrong." If someone is down, it is up to them to make them feel better. If something is wrong at the job-site, it's up to them to solve it and get it right. (Even if it's really not their responsibility.). They will let everyone else off the hook except themselves. On the other hand, because they were made to feel everything was their fault, they may go to the other extreme and be responsible for nothing. They might not take care of themselves physically or be able to hold a steady job. Making decisions and following through on things seems like an insurmountable task to them, so they give up.

Who Gets Hooked and Why

It's often hard for someone to see the manipulation and abuse of the Movement while they are still part of it.(Remember, they're trained to "not see" or call attention to problems.). Once they leave, it becomes more clear to them. Then they wonder how they could ever let themselves be "taken in" like that. They might feel embarrassed and humiliated. If you know someone who has left the Movement, you may wonder the same thing. How could this intelligent person be talked into following a cult?

Many people are attracted to the Boston Movement because they love God and their roots are already in the Restoration Movement. They visit a Boston church and they hear enthusiastic singing. They hear persuasive speaking. They see caring people talking with one another and sharing Scriptures together. They see a church that is concerned about the lost and dedicated to "restoring" New Testament Christianity. They make instant friendships with people their age who want to include them in everything. Their faith seems to become "real" here and they are hooked.

Many of Boston's converts have abusive backgrounds that set them up for further abuse in Boston. Maybe they had a long history of substance abuse. Or were involved in various forms of immorality. Maybe their family of origin ignored their emotional needs. Maybe there was alcoholism, parental absence and neglect, violence, or a broken home. Maybe they were responsible for raising their brothers and sisters (or themselves) when they should have enjoyed being carefree. At Boston they will feel a sense of love, worth, and acceptance they have not had anywhere else — at first. They may be looking for a parental figure to help them and be drawn to the discipleship relationships. Here the same cycle of abuse they experienced before will be played again.

Others are drawn to Boston because they want solutions. They want heroes. Boston can supply both. Her leaders seem strong and powerful. They have answers to life's problems and know the "how-to's" of living a holy life. They have creative and innovative programs. They are excited about the "kingdom of God" and they are visionaries. They are willing to provide guidance and direction to anyone who feels powerless or uncertain.

Those who join the Boston Movement are not the "losers" in life nor do they necessarily lack education. On the contrary, I have known several doctors, lawyers, architects, and others with advanced degrees who endorse this movement. These are not people whose simplicity is being taken advantage of by another. Just the opposite is true. What is being taken advantage of is their desire to please God.

They may have enough Bible knowledge to know something is Biblical, like discipling or confessing sin, but may not know enough to discern error. They may have a vague feeling that something is not quite right, but don't know what it is. (They're usually too tired or too busy to study it out). For instance, they might understand from reading Acts that some of the New Testament Christians sold their homes or possessions and gave the money to the church to distribute to the needy. But, they may have overlooked the fact that none of the apostles ever demanded people to do this! It's the "element of truth" in Boston's teachings that keeps the "hook" in someone. (As a side note, each generation of Boston converts appears to be weaker and weaker Biblically because so much time and energy is focused on performance and not on Bible study.).

If the Boston churches are the first (or only) churches where they've heard teaching on discipleship, evangelism, or commitment, they may tend to stay with the Movement longer because there seems to be no other church that even looks at these areas. So they stay with "the program" and decide to try to glean the good from the bad. They keep mental notes and tell themselves they will not repeat the same abuses when they "go full time." Some apprehension remains however; on the one hand, they feel the Movement is right, but on the other hand, they aren't so sure. The unanswered question for them is, if this (Movement) isn't of God, than what is it? And where is God?

What God Has to Say

"...I am against the shepherds and I will hold them responsible for what has happened to my flock...I will save my flock from being taken for their food. I will search and find my   sheep. I will be like a shepherd looking for his flock. I will find my sheep and rescue them from all the places they were scattered in that dark and cloudy day... I myself will be the Shepherd of my sheep, and cause them to lie down in peace... I will seek my lost ones, those who strayed away, and bring them safely home again. I will put splints and bandages upon their broken limbs and heal the sick. And I will destroy the powerful, fat shepherds..."   *Ezekiel 34: 10-16 LB*

It is next to impossible to recover from the abuses of the Boston Movement without first understanding who God really is. I was stuck at this point for quite awhile. Ex-Boston members don't usually have a *heart* understanding of grace. They know salvation is the gift of God, but in their mind, it comes COD (cash on delivery). There is no sense of freedom and joy involved in their understanding of grace unless they're "doing the things that please God." They hope God loves them, but they are not *convinced* He even likes them, much less cares about them.

Let's take a look first at how God feels about the wounded sheep. Please stop and reread the passage above from Ezekiel. (If you can, read the whole chapter in your Bible.) It's a beautiful picture of God's heart. He feels deeply for His people and is concerned with how they are led. He is moved to action when they are "ruled with force and cruelty" (v.4). He says He will be like a "shepherd looking for his flock." (v.12). He will find them and rescue them wherever they are. If they have broken bones, He will fix them; if they're sick, He will heal them; if they are lost, He will bring them home. He will deal with the bad shepherds, but His foremost concern and priority are finding the wandering sheep. He wants them to "lie down in peace and feed in luscious mountain pastures. I myself will be the Shepherd of my sheep, and cause them to lie down in peace..." (v.14-16).

God's love didn't end with Ezekiel. Both Matthew and Mark describe Jesus looking at the crowds and said "he had compassion on them, because they were harassed and helpless, *like sheep without a shepherd.*" (Matt. 9:36; Mk. 6:34 NIV).

God gives us many illustrations of Himself in the Bible, but I believe His favorite one is the picture of the good shepherd. There are over 30 references throughout the Bible where He refers to His care as that of a shepherd caring for His sheep! The "shepherd theme" is woven throughout the Bible.

("Shepherds" and "shepherding" is mentioned over 200 times!) Two men who were exceptionally close to God, Moses ("the Lord spoke to Moses face to face, as a man speaks to his friend." Ex. 33:11) and David ("...a man after God's own heart..." Acts 13:22), were shepherds. One of the most well known Psalms, Psalm 23, is "The Lord is my shepherd." The angels invited shepherds to witness the virgin birth of God's son. Jesus had compassion like a shepherd. He says "the good shepherd lays down his life for the sheep..." (Jn. 10:14). Peter told the elders to "Be shepherds of God's flock...and when the Chief Shepherd appears, you will receive the crown of life..."(1 Peter 5:2,4) And in Rev. 7:17, "For the Lamb standing in front of the throne will feed them and be their Shepherd and lead them to the springs of the Water of Life. And God will wipe their tears away."

In the Biblical days sheep represented wealth. They were a symbol of prosperity. But as people learned to cultivate crops and build cities, shepherds were no longer respected quite so highly. No one wanted the job so shepherding the sheep was usually assigned to the youngest member of the family, to slaves, or to women. It was considered a lowly job and some people wouldn't even associate with shepherds.

Sheep need the shepherds to take care of them or they will die. They need to be led to pastures and streams so they can be nourished and refreshed. They need someone to give them relief from insects and parasites. They need someone to protect them from their predators. "Sheep" is a fitting symbol for us. We are just like sheep; we need someone else to led us and take care of us or we will die.

The comparison doesn't stop with our need for a shepherd. Just like society in Biblical times considered sheep a symbol of wealth, so God looks at us as His sheep and considers Himself wealthy! *We* are His wealth! "The Lord your God has chosen you out of all the peoples on the face of the earth to be his people, *his treasured possession.*" (Deut. 7:6, also Deut.14:2, 26:18; Ex. 19:5; Ps. 135:4 NIV). "...whoever touches you touches *the apple of his eye...*" (Zech. 2:8; also, Ps. 17:8; Deut. 32:10 NIV). "...We have become *gifts to God* that *he delights in...*" (Eph. 1:11 LB).

God is not ashamed to be our shepherd. It is not a lowly job to Him because He loves us. He loves being the "Great Shepherd of the sheep." (Heb. 13:20). We just have to listen for His voice and follow His lead.

The Purpose of the Law

As stated earlier, one of the leading characteristics of the Boston Movement is her legalism. This can be a major roadblock for ex-members if they still carry the weight of the "should's" and "should not's." They may have a rigid schedule and only feel okay about themselves if they maintain the "spiritual disciplines." What they're lacking is an understanding of the "law" and how God uses it.

God gave us the law for three reasons: (1) to show us how far away we have fallen (Rom. 3:19, 20); (2) to convince us we're helpless to fix it (Gal. 3:10-13,19); and (3) to bring us to Himself (Gal. 3:24).

In Gal. 3:24 (NIV), Paul writes, "So the law was put in charge to lead us to Christ that we might be justified by faith." The term "in charge" is translated as "instructor," "guide," "custodian," or "schoolmaster" in other translations. All of these words come from the Greek word, "paidagogos." It means "a guardian or trainer." In the Greek world, wealthy families used the "paidagogos" to make sure the boys arrived at school safely and on time. If they tried to veer off the path to go somewhere else or just got "out of line," the paidagogos was responsible for disciplining them and getting them back on track. The paidagogos wasn't the teacher; they just got the boys where they needed to be so they could learn from the real teacher.

The law is good because it teaches us our need for God but it does not save us. It brings us to Christ because he is our teacher and our salvation. The goal of the law, according to God's plan, is faith in Jesus Christ. "Christ is the end of the law so that there may be righteousness for everyone who believes." (Rom 10:4 NIV). In the Living Bible, Gal. 3:24-27 reads, "The Jewish laws were our teacher and guide until Christ came to give us right standing with God through our faith. But now that Christ has come, we don't need those laws any longer to guard us and lead us to him. For now we are all children of God through faith in Jesus Christ, and we who have been baptized into union with Christ are enveloped by him."

Even our own law keeping (legalism) just serves to show us how far away we have fallen and how much we need God. Legalistic rules are our "paidagogos." As an example, let's say part of my law keeping is reading the Bible for an hour everyday. The first three days I read and feel pretty good about myself and my discipline. But the fourth day gets too hectic and I don't get that hour to read. At the end of the evening, I feel an inner "pop" of the stick on my backside, telling me to get back on the path. Legalists don't get past the "pop" of the stick. They concentrate on walking the right way on the right path so they don't get "popped" again; they end up missing the point.

Receiving a "pop" (guilt pangs) whenever we begin to stray from the path is not a bad thing. It's natural. We need to be conscious of the fact that we are not what God intended us to be. We are sinners. Our goal, however, is not to see how few "pops" we receive; our goal is to get to school! I'm going to receive some "pops" every day of my life because I'm not perfect, but it's not because God is angry with me. Those "pops" remind me that my salvation is from Christ, not from my performance. I don't hang my head in shame anymore because I know my Father loves me and cherishes our relationship, even when I miss a day of Bible reading. It was never the daily reading, the number of people I studied with, or the amount of discipling I did that made me right in His sight; it was His Son's death. However, appreciating the completeness of His sacrifice leads me to want to do all those other good things. The difference is I *want* to do these things (the language of love) because I'm certain of God's acceptance; I no longer feel like I *have* to do certain things (the language of legalism) to get God to like me. Love creates a relationship and legalism creates a religion.

Paul dealt with the issue of legalism in his letter to the Galatians. There was no Greek word for "legalism" in those days, but it can be substituted whenever he talks about the Law. Some Jews were teaching the Galatian Christians they had to be circumcised and follow Jewish laws or they weren't saved. Many Galatians fell for this and Paul responded back immediately. He asked them, "Who has bewitched you?" (Gal. 3:1 NIV) "Bewitched" refers to the "evil eye," a primary mode of witchcraft at that time. The "evil eye" was a witch's spell that slowly sucked the life out of its victim. Following Jewish rules was sucking the life God gave them out of their hearts. Paul asked them, "What has happened to all your joy?" Legalism does that to all its victims. It drowns out the relationship and results in a joyless, burdensome religion.

Here are some excerpts from Galatians 1-5, from the Living Bible.

"I am amazed that you are turning away so soon from God who, in his love and mercy, invited you to share the eternal life he gives through Christ; you are already following a different 'way to heaven,' which really doesn't go to heaven at all. For there is no other way than the one we showed you, you are being fooled by those who twist and change the truth concerning Christ. Let God's curses fall on anyone, including myself, who preaches another way to be saved... we cannot become right with God by obeying our laws, but only by faith in Jesus Christ to take away our sins... that we might be accepted by God because of faith — and not because we have obeyed laws. For no one will ever be saved by obeying them... We are sinners if we start rebuilding the old systems... of trying to be saved by keeping the laws. For it was through reading the Scripture that I came to realize that I could never find God's favor by trying — and failing — to obey the laws. I came to realize that acceptance with God comes by believing in Christ... if trying to obey the laws never gave you spiritual life in the first place, why do you think that trying to obey them now will make you stronger Christians? ...it is clear that no one can ever win God's favor by trying to keep the laws because God has said that the only way we can be right in his sight is by faith... but Christ has bought us out from under the doom of that impossible system by taking the curse for our wrongdoing upon himself... So Christ has made us free... Christ is useless to you if you are counting on clearing your debt to God by keeping those laws... But we by the help of the Holy Spirit are counting on Christ's death to clear away our sins and make us right with God. And we to whom Christ has given eternal life don't need to worry about whether we... are obeying the Jewish ceremonies or not; for all we need is faith working through love..."

When we understand how completely loved and accepted we are in Christ, legalism will lose its death grip. The chains will drop away and we will no longer be its prisoners. God gave us the law so we would know we can't earn His favor by keeping them. He gave us His Son so He could accept us the same way He accepts His first born.

"We who have been made holy *by Jesus* now have the *same Father* he has. That is why Jesus is *not ashamed to call us his brothers.* For he says in the book of Psalms, 'I will talk to *my brothers* about God my Father, and *together* we will sing his praises... I will put my trust in God along with my *brothers...* See, here am I and *the children God gave me.*'" (Heb. 2:11-13 LB)

"So now there is no condemnation for those who are in Christ Jesus..." (Rom. 8:1 NIV). Notice this does not say, "there is no condemnation for those who are consistently evangelistic; for those who read the Bible for an hour every morning; for those who sacrifice sleep to serve the brotherhood; or for those who sell their house to give money for a church planting. Jesus lifted the heavy weight of the law from our shoulders and we are no longer condemned by it because He already was.

"Long ago, even before he made the world, God chose us to be his very own, through what Christ would do for us; he decided then to make us holy in his eyes, without a single fault — we who stand before him covered with his love. His unchanging plan has always been to adopt us into his own family by sending Jesus Christ to die for us. And he did this because he wanted to!... God is so rich in mercy; he loved us so much that even though we were spiritually dead and doomed by our sins, he gave us back our lives again when he raised Christ from the dead — only by his undeserved favor have we ever been saved — and lifted us up from the grave into glory along with Christ, where we sit with him in the heavenly realms — all because of what Christ Jesus did. And now God can always point to us as examples of how very, very rich his kindness is, as shown in all he has done for us through Jesus Christ. Because of his kindness you have been saved through trusting Christ. And even trusting is not of yourselves; it too is a gift from God. Salvation is not a reward for the good we have done, so none of us can take any credit for it. It is God himself who has made us what we are and given us new lives from Christ Jesus; and long ages ago he planned that we should spend these lives in helping others..." (Eph. 1:4-5; 2:4-10 NIV).

For the One Helping

1) The most important thing to do is to pray for that individual; not just "Lord be with so-and-so," but really talk to God about that person and his situation. Talk to Him just like He was there face to face with you. Tell God how you feel, how the other person feels, what your thoughts are and ask for guidance and wisdom. God will answer that prayer and teach you what to do. When you're talking with that person, ask God, "How can I best encourage and strengthen this person right now?" He will show you.

2) The wounded often need a time to rest before they can recover. They are totally drained (and maybe in shock depending on how they left) and may need physical rest before they can recover mentally, emotionally or spiritually. Most of Boston's members have not had a regular sleep pattern since they joined the Movement. If they recently left the Movement they may need to put a little time between themselves and the wounds they have received. The time will help them step back and separate themselves from Boston. Go very slowly if they recently left, are thinking about leaving, or appear to be "dazed."

3) More than anything else, at any stage they are in, they need to experience unconditional love and acceptance from you. They first felt acceptance from the Boston churches because they were a "baptismal candidate." After that, they were praised for numbers and scolded for poor performance. All they need to know from you is that you love them and they are important to you regardless if they continue with God or not. They need to know there are no strings attached to your friendship.

4) The wounded need to set the pace and start the process towards healing. It can't be hurried or done any other way. They must take the first steps. They cannot just "get over it." You can, however, let them know what you are willing to do for them. You can offer to talk, to pray together or to read the Bible, but emphasize it is okay if they decline. (It might feel like pressure to them). They were taught they are not okay if they do not follow someone's suggestion and they need the permission to say no. Once the offer is made, you will not need to offer it again; just leave the door open and the decision up to them. They may not accept it, but they will not forget it. When they are ready to take the risk of seeking God and/or developing a relationship with a Christian, they will pick the one who is the least threatening and the most accepting.

5) Keep communication honest. Because you're not sure what to say or when to say it, tell them so! Say, "I'm afraid to ask you such-and-such because I don't want you to feel forced into doing something you don't want to do..." They need to see how you're trying to be sensitive to them and giving them room to say no without suffering consequences. (Like withdrawal of the relationship if they don't attend church). Ask questions like, "Would it be okay if...," or " How does this feel to you?" but realize they may not know their feelings since they spent so much time denying them. They are not used to having someone care about what they think or feel. You may need to help them recognize what they're feeling by putting a name to it for them (This is anger, this is grief, etc.), or by telling them how you would feel if you were in a similar experience. ("If someone said/did that to me, I'd be hurt.") The most important needs to humans — the need for love, acceptance and importance — has been unmet in their lives. They were shamed for even having these needs. However, when these needs are met, through God's Word and the care of His people, they will blossom.

6) Your trustworthiness and sincerity will be tested. They will look for hidden motives in your friendship and watch how you are with other people. They want to be sure you do not see them as a "spiritual trophy." They fear manipulation and have a great inside "radar" that detects insincerity. (Tell them you need to earn their trust; they don't have to give it blindly.) They might skip a service or a study to see what your reaction will be. They will watch to see if you are a person of your word, even when it's not convenient. Can you keep appointments, are you on time, can you keep confidences, do you fulfill your promises? If you don't come through on something, they will be greatly interested in how you handle it. Do you apologize? Does it bother you when you can't keep a promise? Do you turn the situation around by telling them they shouldn't be upset if you're late, or if you forget to do something? (Remember they were not allowed to be upset with any leader for any reason, regardless if they should be or not!) What they are doing is "checking out the water." They're sticking their toes in to see if the water is cold or if it's comfortable for swimming. This is a good thing, even if it's somewhat hard for you. They are trying to reassure themselves that you (and/or the church) is a safe place. They are looking for a sense of security before they jump in.

7) Understand that any personal sharing (doesn't have to be connected with Boston) will be a big risk for them to take. The struggles they shared with the Movement leaders were usually used against them, so they will be careful with what they disclose about themselves now. If they do share a personal item with you, they're past the toes and now they're putting their foot in the

water. This is a good sign! Let them know you understand it was probably hard for them to be vulnerable and you are glad they entrusted that part of themselves to you. Then you can rejoice because it is a signal that you have passed, or are soon to pass, the "trust test."

8) Be ready for emotional explosions of anger, hurt, resentment, bitterness, and grief as they begin to heal from their past abuses. Don't be afraid of it (the emotions) and don't feel you must solve it for them because you can't. The raw emotions are coming about because they're seeing the Movement as it really is and they are responding to it accordingly. These feelings are stuffed down and held tightly but must be released if they are to heal. They may be reluctant to "burden" anyone with this, but sooner or later, it must be discussed with someone. They may be like a pressure cooker. The farther away they get from the Movement, the more clearly they will see how they have been used. They will be angry with those who betrayed their trust and ashamed that they were so deceived by the Movement. They think others will think they are "stupid." At this point, the most important thing you can do is just listen. Let them get it out. You will need to say very few words; just accepting them (through listening) says it all. You may hear stories you find hard to believe and it may be painful for you to listen. As they talk about things they may never have shared before, they will feel like they are "throwing up." It may take awhile for them to get it all out, so be patient. (I also used journals and sometimes a tape recorder if I was driving to release the pent up emotions.) Avoid making judgments or showing opinions, just hear them out. That will be a brand new experience for them.

9) Help them find professional help if needed. You may not be equipped to handle certain issues they may have. If there is any physical, emotional, or sexual abuse in their past (in or outside the Boston Movement), if they are willing, help them find a trustworthy counselor who is trained and experienced with these matters. This is important because they may have a background that sets them up to be abused and they don't realize it. If so, these are better handled by someone trained to do so. In the meanwhile, they need to know you are not shutting them out, so continue to be there for them in whatever way you can, but don't get overwhelmed with their pain.

10) When they are ready to read the Bible again, sometimes reading a translation other than the one the Movement uses makes a difference. It did for me. Whenever I would read the New International Version (NIV), the old tapes connected with that particular passage kept rolling through my mind and I would feel condemned all over again. I switched to the Phillips translation, the Living Bible and the Message before I read NIV again. The

different translations opened my eyes and it was like reading a passage for the first time. (For most people, one different translation will be enough!) I focused on the four Gospels and read them continually until I felt comfortable with who Jesus was. Once I had a grasp of what God was like, reading the rest of the New Testament was not difficult. It wasn't the list of rules and commands I once thought it was; it was — dare I say it? — enjoyable!

11) Help them learn good Bible study methods. One of Boston's (really, Kip McKean's) problems is that she/he reads the New Testament through Old Testament eyes. She builds the church based on Old Testament situations (like the "Jethro" advice and the rebuilding of Jerusalem by Nehemiah) instead of the book of Acts and the rest of the New Testament. McKean believes the book of Judges is a guidebook on leadership and encourages his people to study it for that purpose. The ex-member **must** learn how to put things into **context** and to read all the Scriptures on a subject before they draw definite conclusions. It may be as simple as asking questions like "Who was this written to? Why was it written? What were the surrounding circumstances? What were the writer's feelings?" Take a look at the Bible and reference material they are using. Are they easy for them to use and understand? Would a different Bible or reference book be more useful? A study Bible like the Life Application series and commentaries are a big help. They may need to learn how to use dictionaries and other reference books to gain further understanding about the Hebrew and Greek meanings of words or the customs of the times.

12) They will need help in understanding God's nature. For them to make the choice to trust God, their view of God will need a major overhaul until they believe in their heart what they know in their minds. The largest gap any of us need to bridge is the gap between our mind and our heart and this is no less true for ex-Boston members. Remember, they know with their minds that salvation is by grace, but their heart may not really believe it. When they are ready to read the Bible, study every passage possible about grace. Understanding grace, from the heart, will take care of nearly every issue in their life, because most of their problems stem from how they view God! Show them passages where God confronts spiritual abuse, either through Jesus, the apostles, or the prophets. Study passages that explain God's heart and describe His love for His people. Help them see how He shows His loving character throughout the Scriptures and in our lives. Share what God means to you and how you see Him working in your life. Help them see God as our source and the Body of Christ as the resource.

13) They may need some major doctrinal help. Because they were so thoroughly taught to trust leadership, they may have trouble comparing the Boston teachings with Biblical teaching on their own. At the same time, they may be afraid to ask you for help because they don't want to be led astray again. You need to be extra patient with them as they wrestle with the "truth" of their former teachings, especially in the areas of autonomy, discipleship, baptism, and authority. Help them study out their false teachings and assumptions without too much "spoon feeding." (They might need this in the beginning, but be sure they go back and reread the Scriptures on their own). They are afraid of letting go of their previous beliefs, even if they truly want to because their "programming" tells them God will leave them if they forsake the Movement's beliefs. To leave it behind (i.e., the movement) takes a firm and confident understanding of the Scriptures and the power of God. Be careful they do not throw out the good and proper teaching with the bad. For instance, once they see how deeply they were controlled by other Christians, they may reject the idea of discipleship altogether. Help them balance it.

14) They may compare everything they see to the good in the church they left — and feel disappointed. They may be looking for the same dynamic preaching, the same level of commitment, and the same enthusiastic worship service that attracted them to Boston and not be able to find it. They are usually looking for the same exact church as Boston, but without the abuses. The comparison may be unconscious, but it is usually there. They need to accept that there is no perfect church.

15) Help them experience and understand what a healthy church (or, safe system) is. In a healthy church, mistakes and disagreements still occur, but the difference is they can talk about it. Having problems does not kill the church; not talking about them does! Help them see it is okay to question or to disagree, to express their feelings and to be who they are. Show them that in a healthy church, glorifying Jesus is the focus, not the minister or the movement. Show them that equality is stressed, not a hierarchy or submission (Eph. 5:21; Gal. 3:28). Let them know God gave each of us different (meaning not the same) gifts to help and strengthen each other.

16) Have them take a personality test so they can see what their natural strengths and weaknesses are. Point out to them that each personality type has inherent strengths and weaknesses. This will also help you understand them more and how to help them.

17) Certain "buzz" words, like accountability, commitment, dealing with sin and so on may cause a panic attack because of their association with the

Movement. Be sure to clarify what you mean and allow them to ask questions if you think you have hit upon a mine field. (You may have to bring up the question you think they have. Ex — "Are you afraid the discipleship groups will humiliate you or think less of you if you have a bad week? Or if you don't read all of the next chapter?")

18) If available, introduce them to someone who has also left the Movement. This will take some pressure off you and give them another resource person. It will give them more confidence because they can see others who have "made it through" as well as someone who empathizes with their plight.

19) Help them stay out of the victim mentality. They cannot change the fact that the abuse happened, but they can decide how they will react to the hurt. That is *their* responsibility and only they can take it. You may have to remind them of this from time to time after they have worked through the initial stages. Once they have taken the risks to go on, they can look back at the past and learn to make better choices, without blaming the way life is now on something in the past. In time they will be able to look back, see the abuse and not wish vengeance on the abuser. This takes time and growth; it doesn't happen all at once or even at one point in time. It does eventually happen as long as they do not think of themselves as helpless victims or hold onto the anger.

20) Don't let all of your conversation and relationship center on the Boston Movement. There will be times when the Movement monopolizes some talks, but it shouldn't be always. Do some fun activities and talk about "non-spiritual" things as well; let them see you and themselves as "real people."

21) As the trust in your relationship grows, ask more and more questions that make them think. This will be difficult for them at first, but will help them stand on their own so to speak. Ask them questions about themselves, like their hobbies, likes and dislikes, family background, vacation plans and so on. Ask them about their experiences in the Movement like, how'd you feel when he said that, when that was done to you, what was going on in your life when you were first approached by a member and invited to church? Ask questions to find out how they came to certain conclusions. This is as important to you as it is to them. They need to be able to examine their thought and decision making processes to uncover their false beliefs and assumptions. This is "mind renewal."

22) It won't always be this hard for them or you! When they first begin to deal with the Movement and their relationship with God, the progress may seem like a snail's pace with a Herculean amount of effort, but it won't stay

that way. Recovery from any abuse is tough work and healing is always a process. However, once the roots of God's love begin to take hold of them, the nagging voices of doubt and suspicion will fade away, and they will blossom!

For the Ex-Boston Member

It took courage for you to leave the Boston Movement and it's going to take courage for you to rebuild your faith. Courage is not the absence of fear; it's *in spite* of fear. You're going to feel afraid, confused, and lost, but keep going towards the goal. Healing is a process; it takes time. It's not going to happen overnight, but it doesn't have to take forever.

When I decided to seek God again, I prayed daily that He would help me see His loving nature and help me trust Him. I told Him I felt like I was playing "Blind Man's Bluff" and I was stumbling around in the dark, unable to find Him. I knew I couldn't do this unless He helped me. God answered my prayers. There was no single moment where the clouds suddenly disappeared and the light clicked on. In His wisdom, He knew I would not be able to handle that type of "zing." He gave me the type and amount of food I was able to digest at each stage of my "seeker" stage. Even though I believe God was gentle in leading me back to Him, it wasn't easy or painless. It won't be for you either. As you travel your own road to recovery, you may feel intense pain and hurt as memories are re-stirred and wounds uncovered. Don't be afraid of it or try to push it down because it's all part of the process. It won't always hurt.

Allow yourself time to grieve. You have been lied to and deceived by those you trusted. You will feel a sense of loss — of time, of innocence, of money, of friends, of support, of love, and of goodness. You may feel depressed and not know why; it may be because you're mourning what you have lost. This is a good, although painful, part of the recovery process. As you step back and get a clearer view of the Movement, you may feel this sense of loss more acutely, but it won't last forever. It won't swallow you.

Understanding the Boston Movement as it really is — a religious cult — may help you in the healing process. When I wrote the first draft of this book, my understanding of cults was limited to various images I gleaned from the media of long robes, shaved heads, and communal living.

Although I believed Boston to be "on the fringe," I hesitated to call it a cult because it seemed, well, overdramatic. After all, in all of my experience with Boston, I was never required to solicit donations in airports, sell candy, burn incense, or chant endlessly.

My superficial understanding of cultic groups was challenged when I read the following list of common cult characteristics written by Dr. Michael D. Langone, executive director of the American Family Foundation.

Checklist of Cult Characteristics (by Dr. Michael Langone)[1]

* The group is focused on a living leader to whom members seem to display excessively zealous, unquestioning commitment.

* The group is preoccupied with bringing in new members.

* The group is preoccupied with making money.

* Questioning, doubt, and dissent are discouraged or even punished.

* Mind-numbing techniques (such as meditation, chanting, speaking in tongues, denunciation sessions, debilitating work routines) are used to suppress doubts about the group and its leader(s).

* The leadership dictates — sometimes in great detail — how members should think, act, and feel (for example: members must get permission from leaders to date, change jobs, get married; leaders may prescribe what types of clothes to wear, where to live, how to discipline children and so forth).

* The group is elitist, claiming a special, exalted status for itself, its leader(s) and members.

* The group has a polarized us-versus-them mentality, which causes conflict with the wider society.

* The group's leader is not accountable to any authorities. The group teaches or implies that its supposedly exalted ends justify means that members would have considered unethical before joining the group.

* The leadership induces feelings of guilt in members in order to control them.

* Members' subservience to the group causes them to cut ties with family, friends, and personal group goals and activities that were of interest before joining the group.

* Members are expected to devote inordinate amounts of time to the group.

* Members are encouraged or required to live and/or socialize only with other members.

Dr. Margaret Singer, a leading expert on cults, identified other characteristics of cults and cult leaders:[2]

* Cults are authoritarian in their power structure.

* Cults tend to be totalitarian in their control of the behavior of the members.

* Cults tend to have double sets of ethics; one for the leader and another for the members.

* Cult leaders are self-appointed and claim to have a special mission in life.

* Cult leaders tend to be charismatic, determined, and domineering.

* Cult leaders center the veneration (worship, admiration) of members upon themselves.

* Cults appear to be innovative and exclusive.

* Cults basically have two purposes: recruiting new members and fund-raising.

As I read through this list of characteristics and thought about the traits I had already written about with the Boston Movement, I realized that if I interchanged "Boston Movement" for "cults," this list would stay pretty much intact. I continued to read more information about cults and am now convinced that the Boston Movement, or International Church of Christ, is indeed a cult.

As a friend of mine says, "If it walks like a duck and talks like a duck..."

Defining "cult"

The American Family Foundation defines a cult as: "A group or movement exhibiting great or excessive devotions or dedication to some person, idea, or thing, and employing unethical manipulative or coercive techniques of persuasion and control, designed to advance the goals of the group's leaders, to the actual or possible detriment of members, their families, or the community." The unethical techniques used include isolation from former friends and family, debilitation, use of special methods to heighten suggestibility and subservience, powerful group pressures, information management, suspension of individuality or critical judgment, promotion of total dependency on the group and fear of leaving it.[3]

Dr. Langone distinguishes three characteristics that identify cultic groups from other groups.

1) Members are expected to be excessively zealous and unquestioning in their commitment to the identity and leadership of the group. 2) Members are manipulated and exploited. 3) Harm or the threat of harm may come to members, their families, and/or society.[3]

In their book, *Captive Minds, Captive Hearts*, Madeleine Tobias and Janja Lalich discuss the cultic relationship. They say it is not the size of a group that defines a cult, but their behavior. It can be large or it can be one-on-one.

"The one-on-one cult is based in the belief in one's partner or teacher above all else. Generally an intimate relationship is used to manipulate and control the partner or student, who believes the dominant one to have special knowledge or special powers... There is a significant power imbalance between the two participants. The stronger uses his or her influence to control, manipulate, abuse, and exploit the other. In essence the cultic relationship is a one-on-one version of the larger group. It may even be more intense than participation in a group cult since all the attention and abuse is focused on one person, often with damaging consequences..."[4]

If you have never seen a list of cultic characteristics, reading this may have sent a shock wave through your system. Or, as it did me, maybe you feel a sense of relief because you can place a name on your experiences. The Boston Movement has many of the characteristics common to cults. The Movement centers around Kip McKean and his followers (i.e., disciplers) nearly worship him. No one can be the "ultimate example" in every area of life, yet his disciples believe he is. They all want to be "just like Kip." McKean tells others to publicly praise their disciplers, but he has never admitted to wanting to be "just like" someone else. Those close to him aren't sure who he answers to either. In a radio interview, Al Baird could list who was being discipled by whom, but when he was asked who discipled Kip McKean, he said, "Kip reports to, to — uh — I don't know — no one." Later in the conversation he said, "Who does the pope report to?"[5]

Just like other cults, Boston cuts off the flow of information from the "outside" to her members. People are marked for disloyalty, emotionalism, and even for sentimentality and no one is allowed to talk with these former members. McKean calls criticism "spiritual pornography." He and other top leaders don't allow members to read or watch anything negative towards their Movement. They revise their history and color the facts of retention rate and membership to reflect what they want. (Some membership growth is due to dismantling a church and telling the members to attend a certain other church; in Denver, McKean stated that Boston had a 90% retention rate her first year and 70% over her nine years and wrote in an article that it was about 50% — see Jones, *WDTBMT?* Vol.3, p.33).

If Boston is truly based on the New Testament, then Acts should be filled with re-baptisms and reconstruction of churches, but it's not. When churches were doing poorly, the leaders weren't demoted and sent back to Jerusalem for retraining. The apostles never appointed church leaders and evangelists for other churches; the church voted on her own local leadership. Each New Testament church selected her own elders to oversee her. (Only two churches in all of the Boston Movement has elders).

There is no need to rehash all that's already been said about the pressure and the rules and the drive for more baptisms. You know all this. Feelings, emotions, and opinions are down-played except for the ones the leaders wanted you to have. You were required to confess every thought, action, or word and they used the knowledge of your inner-self against you. They constantly reminded you of your weaknesses, your fears, and your vulnerabilities so they could control you. These are traits of cults *and* of the Boston Movement.

Most people feel humiliated to say they were "duped" by a cult. It doesn't mean you're stupid or crazy; it just means someone took advantage of your innocence and your vulnerability. All cults operate in the same way, which is why it can be documented, books are written about it, and counselors are trained to help those who have been affected by them.

Cults — and the Boston Movement is no exception — operate in three basic steps. They "deprogram" you by convincing you that everything you've learned prior to the group is wrong. They isolate you from your past life. Then they break down your will to become theirs and "reprogram" you to think exactly what they want you to think. Mind control is real, powerful, and subtle. You are not the first or the last person to be seduced.

After reading this, you may be even more afraid of developing relationships or entering a church door again! You don't have to be if you use your experience to your betterment, not as a defensive mechanism.

Beginning the Healing Process

No one can make you "better." You must take ownership of that responsibility. That doesn't mean you have to do it alone, it just means *you* decide when and how to deal with your hurts and your faith. There are people who can help you, but recovery is up to you. Since you're reading this, I will assume you have made the choice to heal.

Take a realistic look at the Movement. Use a journal, tape recorder, and/or discuss it with a friend. (You'll probably do a combination of these). Write down your autobiography while part of the Movement. Let whatever comes up, come up. This may bring up painful memories, but hang with it. Rereading it will help you be more objective about what happened and clearer on some of the dynamics. If you need to, educate yourself on cults and mind controlling techniques. You should be able to find some good books in your local library.

Read the Bible and talk to God. Talk to other Christians if you can. Take it at your pace and don't worry about what you think they think. God (and healthy churches) will respect your boundaries. God is not bothered by our questions, our fears, or our doubts. He welcomes them because He can heal and put you on solid rock. I started reading the Bible a couple of years before I attended church so I could develop my own idea of God. Then I started to check out churches and visited the one I eventually joined for nearly a year before I began any relationships. This worked for me although I wouldn't necessarily recommend it for everyone. It prolonged my own recovery process because I wouldn't talk to anyone and did most of my "work" alone. However, you be the judge of what will work for you in your process; there are no rules written in stone. It will most likely change as you go because your needs will change as you grow.

When I began to read the Bible, I stayed away from the NIV (New International Version) because it was the "Bible of choice" in the Movement. I found whenever I read the NIV, certain passages would trigger the guilt provoking sermons/teachings associated with it by the Movement. Instead, I read the Living Bible, the Philips' translation, and the Message. I would recommend any of these to you. I also used a highlighter system when I read. All the verses connected with the cross were highlighted in orange, sin was blue, and God's nature was yellow. Whenever I would feel scared of God, I would flip through the pages and read the yellow highlighted passages. There are quite a few.

Get to know God. Study grace and if you're having a hard time understanding it, get someone you've learned to trust to help you. Apply the truth to your mind and let it soak into your heart. Your conscience will judge you according to what *it* thinks is right or wrong, so teach yourself the truth. Renew your mind through the Bible. In Rev. 12:10,11, we are told that Satan accuses us night and day before God, but we overcome him by the blood of the Lamb. Tell yourself the truth every time Boston memories stand up to accuse you. The best way not to be deceived by cults or manipulative people is by knowing the truth and by knowing God. God's people will reflect God. As you know, He does not force His way upon you or tell you to follow blindly.

Reject the temptation to "throw out the baby with the bath water." As said earlier, there is an element of truth in many of Boston's teachings, so don't reject the whole concept just because Boston misapplied it. As you study the Bible and learn to read the whole picture, you'll understand the difference. Discussing this with other Christians will help you discern truth from error too.

As you search out a church home and Christian friends, remember that not all churches are like Boston. Not every leader is out to use you. Remember that you have "rights" to boundaries. You don't have to disclose things about yourself that you're not ready to talk about. You don't have to give 100% blind loyalty and trust. Trust is a process, not a command.

As you continue in your healing and your growth, be sure you forgive those in your past who hurt you. Don't allow the anger to develop into bitterness and revenge. Understand, however, that this takes time. First you have to give yourself time to grieve and to release the anger. (For me, this included journal writing and role playing with the help of a counselor). Ask God to help you to forgive because you cannot manufacture it on your own. Secondly, understand that forgiveness (of yourself and those who hurt you) will probably come in stages. It's unlikely that you will forgive everyone for everything all at once, but you should see some progress with this as you go along. Remember, the damage you received didn't happen all at one time and neither will the healing.

For a long time, my view of God was similar to the way the one talent man felt towards his master in Matt. 25. I was afraid that when I faced God, He would be angry with how I lived my life on earth. I was always trying to see what "more" I should be doing so I wouldn't disappoint God and be ashamed of myself. Then I read this passage:

"We know how much God loves us because we have felt his love and because we believe him when he tells us that he loves us dearly. God is love and anyone who lives in love is living with God and God is living in him. And as we live with Christ, our love grows more perfect and complete; so we will not be ashamed and embarrassed at the day of judgment, but can face him with confidence and joy, because he loves us and we love him too. We need have no fear of someone who loves us perfectly; his perfect love for us eliminates all dread of what he might do to us. If we are afraid, it is for fear of what he might do to us, and shows that we are not fully convinced that he really loves us. So you see, our love for him comes as a result of his loving us first." (1 John 4:16-19 LB).

If you do nothing else, bathe yourself in God's love. That will bring changes in your heart and mind that you can only dream of now. All of our Christian life is learning to walk consistently with who we are in Christ. You won't do it perfectly, but you can draw closer to God day by day and it will overflow to others.

In Ephesians 1:13; 2 Cor. 1:22; and 2 Cor. 5:5, we are told that we were "sealed with the Holy Spirit" as a "guarantee" that He will bring us to Himself (v.14). The Greek word for "guarantee" is "arrabon." It means "engagement ring." God gave us His Spirit as an engagement ring! What does that mean? It means He wants us to be with Him! Let your mind dwell on that thought for awhile.

I'd like to close this booklet with a couple of Scriptures because they say what is really necessary for us to know:

"And now just as you trusted Christ to save you, trust him, too, for each day's problems; live in vital union with him. Let your roots grow down into him and draw up nourishment from him. See that you go on growing in the Lord, and become strong and vigorous in the truth you were taught. Let your lives overflow with joy and thanksgiving for all he has done." (Col. 2:6,7 LB)

"He is able to save completely all who come to God through him. Since he will live forever, he will always be there to remind God that he has paid for their sins with his blood." (Heb. 7:25 LB)

"For it is from God alone that you have your life through Christ Jesus. He showed us God's plan of salvation; he was the one who made us acceptable to God; he made us pure and holy and gave himself to purchase our salvation. As it says in the Scriptures, 'If anyone is going to boast, let him boast only of what the Lord has done.'" (1 Cor. 1:30-31)

" ...always thankful to the Father who has made us fit to share all the wonderful things that belong to those who live in the kingdom of light..." (Col. 1:12 LB)

"This High Priest of ours understands our weaknesses, since he had the same temptations we do, though he never once gave way to them and sinned. So let us come boldly to the very throne of God and stay there to receive his mercy and to find grace to help us in our times of need." (Heb. 4:15,16 LB)

"Do you think I like to see the wicked die? asks the Lord. Of course not! I only want him to turn from his wicked ways and live." (Eze. 18:23)

"And if under the old system the blood of bulls and goats and the ashes of young cows could cleanse men's bodies from sin, just think how much more surely the blood of Christ will transform our lives and hearts. His sacrifice frees us from the worry of having to obey the old rules, and makes us want to serve the living God. For by the help of the eternal Holy Spirit, Christ willingly gave himself to God to die for our sins — he being perfect, without a single sin or fault. Christ came with this new agreement so that all who are invited may come and have forever all the wonders God has promised them. For Christ died to rescue them from the penalty of the sins they had committed while still under that old system." (Heb. 9:13-15 LB)

"Let us go right in, to God himself, with true hearts fully trusting him to receive us, because we have been sprinkled with Christ's blood to make us clean, and because our bodies have been washed with pure water." (Heb. 10:22 LB)

---

[1] Dr. Michael Langone, *Cults: Questions and Answers,* (Weston, MA: American Family Foundation, 1988). The AFF is an excellent source of help and can be contacted at American Family Foundation, P.O. Box 2265, Bonita Springs, Florida 34133.

[2] Margaret Maler Singer and Janja Lalich, *Cults In Our Midst: The Hidden Menace in Our Everyday Lives.* (San Francisco: Tossey-Bass, 1995).

[3] Dr. Michael Langone, *Cults: Questions and Answers.*

[4] Madeleine Landau Tobias and Janja Lalich, *Captive Hearts, Captive Minds* (Alameda: Hunter House Inc., 1994) pp. 16-17.

[5] Jerry Jones, *WDTBMT?* Vol. 1, p. 39.

Recommended Reading

The Subtle Power of Spiritual Abuse by David Johnson and Jeff VanVonderen (Minneapolis, MN: Bethany House Publishers, 1991).

Healing Spiritual Abuse by Ken Blue (Downers Grove, IL: InterVarsity Press, 1993).

Tired of Trying to Measure Up by Jeff VanVonderen (Minneapolis, MN: Bethany House Publishers, 1989).

Churches That Abuse by Ronald M. Enroth (Grand Rapids, MI: Zondervan, 1992).

When God's People Let You Down by Jeff VanVonderen (Minneapolis, MN: Bethany Publishers, 1994).

What Does the Boston Movement Teach? Vol 1-3 by Jerry Jones
order from: Star Bible Publications
P.O. Box 821220
Fort Worth, TX 76182

Toxic Faith by Stephen Arterburn and Jack Felton (Nashville, TN: Thomas Nelson, 1991).

Captive Hearts, Captive Minds by Madeleine Landau Tobias and Janja Lalich (Alameda, CA: Hunter House, 1994).